The Perfect Capital Campaign

A Guide to Relationship Based Fundraising and Quality Decisions

Schuyler D. Lehman

DEDICATION

I dedicate this book and all the life experience that went into it and to my loving and supportive family – my wife Jennifer, and my four children, Schuyler Jr., Trevor, Ellie and Jack, whose sacrifice of time with me over the years allowed me to pursue my passion for fundraising.

Table of Contents

Introduction

SECTION I – The Philosophy of Quality Decisions

SECTION II – The Perfect Campaign

SECTION III – Cornerstones of Success

Introduction

Books on fundraising are a dime a dozen. I have bought and read far too many of them. When I see another new release, I think, "Not another book about fundraising!" There are hundreds books out there that say the same thing in just a slightly different way. Please, no more books on a new version of "moves management." What more could be said on that? And how much newer could it even get?

I have vowed publicly on a number of occasions not to contribute to the shelves of unread books in the offices of my clients and colleagues. So to now be writing a book on fundraising is a surprise to me to be sure.

With those thoughts now out in the open, let me attempt to explain how I could possibly have changed my position on this matter and actually succumbed to the temptation of adding *author* to my credentials.

Having been in the fundraising world for 30 years, I have soaked up a plethora of experiences and witnessed things that I cannot begin to explain. I have marveled at the strength and resilience of U.S. philanthropy. We are far and away the most generous and giving of cultures on the planet, and our giving continues to be solid in spite of the ups and downs of the economy.

As a consultant to nonprofit organizations for three decades, I have been a road warrior, traveling over 12 million air miles across the 48 contiguous states alone. And I have plenty of battle scars to prove it. My kids are amazed that Dad has been to virtually every major city in our nation—and that we have plenty of frequent flyer points to take our family vacations. You can't help but gain some wisdom living this life. And while many valuable lessons have come from the multitude of clients that I have had the honor of serving, the most important lessons have come from the people who support those clients year after year: the donors.

It is the donors who are largely responsible for my knowledge and philosophy today. And the donors bestowed their wisdom on me without even knowing it.

We fundraising consultants have been so consumed with telling our clients all they should be doing to communicate to their donors that we have a blind spot for the most important perspective: the one perspective that should drive all that we, and the countless nonprofit organizations out there, do to communicate with and strategically nurture donor relationships.

I will never forget the David Letterman stunt back in the early days of his career on *Late Night*. He would strap a camera to a monkey's head and broadcast live as the monkey ran through the studio. It was called the Monkey-Cam, and it gave us perspective from a monkey's eye view. But what made this stunt so interesting was not just that we saw the studio from places only a monkey can go; it was that we actually began looking at things from the mental perspective of the monkey. We wondered, "What must this monkey be thinking as he sees all these things?" Most interesting was when the monkey looked up at humans, and from the perspective of the monkey, people suddenly didn't look all that smart.

So what if we could strap a camera onto the heads of our donors and see what things truly look like from their perspective—the donor's eye view. Before I go any further with this analogy, let me say that I am in no way implying that our donors are monkeys; rather, that maybe we fundraisers don't look as smart as we think we are from the donor's perspective.

Well, my stab at a book is aimed at precisely that: looking at the quality of donor decisions from the donor perspective. I began this empathetic journey with donors many years ago, and it has reshaped my approach to fundraising entirely.

I encourage everyone in the fundraising world (executive director, development staff, board members, etc.) to take time to explore the donors' eye view of your mission and approach to fundraising. It is frightening at first, and the process itself might make you uncomfortable. But it will tell you more about the effectiveness of your efforts than any other means. It is both enlightening and humbling to see things in this light.

My intent with this offering is to give you something new and fresh in regard to fundraising and, specifically, conducting a capital campaign. When you truly analyze the quality of the decisions donors make to support your mission, you can't help but learn. I assure you, seeing fundraising (for capital or operations) from the perspective of the donor will change everything. And putting this philosophy to work on both capital and operations can result in the near perfect harmony among your fundraising activities. Let's dig in.

SECTION I

The Philosophy Behind Quality Decisions

Chapter 1

The Reality of Fundraising

"Too often the shortcut, the line of least resistance, is responsible for evanescent and unsatisfactory results."

—Louis Binstock

Once upon a time, there were two sisters who lived separate and very different lives. Both were single and had no children.

One sister—let's call her Peggy—lived on a remote plot of land miles from any other human beings. Peggy never ventured out into the world to interact with other people. Peggy's entire means of relating to others was by e-mail and social media. Although she had hundreds of online friends, few people had actually met Peggy in person.

The other sister—we'll call her Mary—lived in an apartment in a large metropolitan area. She had three extremely close friends who lived in the adjacent apartments whom she visited in person almost every day. Mary didn't have a computer or cell phone because she saw no need. She got everything she needed from her three friends and had no room for others in her life.

You may not know anyone who is as extreme as Peggy or Mary, but you have probably heard of people like them and wondered how they got that way.

If you had to choose one sister's life over the other, which would you choose? Is it better to have only a few extremely close friends or hundreds of acquaintances with whom you have an arm's length relationship? Which sister would have the most fulfilling life? Which scenario would earn the greatest personal return?

There is not necessarily an easy or correct answer. Both scenarios could easily be sociological case studies. Each sister has something important that the other is lacking. Peggy's life could be described as an inch deep and a mile wide, while Mary has all her eggs in one basket.

The parable of the two sisters depicts two forms of dysfunctional living and neither is correct if representing one's entire relational life. Most people would say that Peggy and Mary are probably both in need of some counseling.

I can't begin to tell you how many nonprofit organizations exist in an environment replicating the relational lives of either Mary or Peggy. They are either relying entirely on the generosity of a few key benefactors who provide nearly all of the funding or relying entirely on mass-marketing strategies to sustain the mission.

The real irony is that the leaders of those nonprofits are not like Mary or Peggy. They are completely reasonable and intelligent people who would almost certainly agree that the parable describes two absurd scenarios.

I have found that most nonprofits have competent and quality leadership, frequently comprised of successful businessmen and businesswomen who have great passion for the mission of the organization. However, for some unknown reason, business sense gets checked at the door as these leaders gather for a board meeting. The woman who is the leading real estate agent in the city is the same person who believes that the best approach to fundraising is to make a soft ask in an end-of-year direct mail piece. The successful executive who has a reputation for negotiating shrewd business deals is the same man who believes that the most effective way to increase fundraising revenue is to host a special event with a silent auction.

Neither of these individuals would dream of running their businesses that way. If they did, they would not have achieved the success that defines them today.

The reality of fundraising is that it is not all that different from the way we function in our personal lives. We all need relationships to be healthy. We need a few close friends with whom we share everything as well as many casual friends and acquaintances we can count on for social gatherings, carpooling, or a cup of sugar. This is the perfect model for a nonprofit fundraising operation.

The depth of the relationship determines the quality of consideration and the decision to support the mission. On the impersonal end of the relational spectrum, casual, transactional decisions are made. Whether you are buying a candy bar in the grocery store checkout lane or dropping loose change into the Ronald McDonald House receptacle at the drive-thru window, these are impulsive decisions that are likely forgotten 30 minutes later. I define these decisions as *transactional*.

On the other end of the relational spectrum, personal and life-impacting decisions are made. It doesn't matter if you are buying a house, a car, or making a sizeable contribution to a nonprofit, the decision-making process is similar. This magnitude of decision involves much more deliberation and discernment. I define these decisions as *transformational*.

The process by which people are brought to decision is very different in each scenario. Although every person is unique and will consider different things based on their passions and interests, it is the relationship and quality of the decision that makes the difference.

At the risk of sounding cliché, building relationships and guiding decisions is the essence of development—the reality of fundraising.

Yet these are the two things that are most commonly scrubbed from most nonprofit funding strategies in an effort to take the path of least resistance.

My favorite is the board member or executive director who determines that the only thing that can be done to help fundraising revenue is prayer—implying that prayer alone will produce money. As a committed and passionate believer in Jesus Christ, I will be the first to advocate prayer for everything that is important in our lives. And prayer in support of fundraising efforts is no exception—I believe it works. Pray, pray some more, and pray again—but don't ignore the logic, planning skills, and intelligence that God gives us all.

I am reminded of the old joke we have all heard many times about the man sitting on the roof of his house in a massive flood, praying to God to be saved. Soon a boat comes by and asks the man to step aboard and be saved from the rising water. He politely declines indicating that he has prayed for God to save him, not a boat. Later, a helicopter hovers over the man offering a way out of the certain doom he will face if he stays on the roof. Again he replies that he is waiting for God to answer his prayers and save him. As the water rises, the man is forced on the top of his chimney with only a matter of minutes before he is overcome by the floodwaters. He unleashes an angry plea to God saying, "Why didn't You save me, I prayed for You to save me!!!" To which God replies, "I sent a boat and helicopter for you. What else can I do?"

I don't ever want to discount the possibility of God performing miracles, for which there are no logical explanations. However, more often than not, God answers prayers through other people. When we pray for a victim of a heart attack, we pray for the skills of the heart surgeon. When we pray for new worship space, we pray for guidance in the selection of an architect. So too should we pray for guidance and new ideas in fundraising.

The lesson of course being, *God works through His people and utilizes every available resource and technology to answer our prayers.*

The reality of fundraising is simply that we tend to take the path of least resistance whenever we think we can get away with it. It is human nature to do so.

As appreciators of wine, my wife and I learn all we can about the art of wine making. While every step of the process is vital to producing a great wine, it is a quality grape that is the foundation. There is no shortcut or path of least resistance to producing a quality grape. In fact, it is critical that the grapevine struggle for survival in order to produce a quality grape. It is the struggle that results in the vine roots reaching down into the soil for all the nutrients it can find to survive. The struggle is what gives the grape its character and flavor.

Character and flavor are the marks of many good things. For example, all relationships require effort and sometimes struggle. Lasting friendships don't usually happen without our willingness to invest effort and risk rejection. It is not always easy, but it is the challenge that often makes friendships great. Likewise, fundraising relationships often take effort and struggle, and it is the often the most challenging relationships that bring the greatest return. There are no shortcuts to lasting fundraising relationships—but the challenge of getting there is what makes the fruit worth every ounce of care.

.

Chapter 2

The Reciprocal Relationship

"To every action there is an equal and opposite reaction."
—Sir Isaac Newton's Third Law of Motion

"For it is in giving that we receive."
—St. Francis of Assisi

"Do unto others as you would have them do unto you."
—*The Golden Rule*

We are bombarded with words of wisdom and sayings throughout our lives about how to treat others. There are hundreds of other quotes and proverbs that instruct us how to behave toward one another in a relationship. Almost all of these quips deal with the reciprocal nature of relationships. Why then is it such a rarity that we find them applied in our charitable giving?

"Human nature is to expect greatness, and do the bare minimum to achieve it."

—Schuyler Lehman

This saying rings true in many aspects of our lives. We want to be all that we can be . . . as long as it doesn't require much effort! For anyone who has reared children, you know well the sense of entitlement that appears in their attitudes. This same perspective is also prevalent in the relationships between nonprofits and their donors.

Why Do You Give?

Let's first establish that we are all philanthropists. Regardless of how much you give, you are a philanthropist. Your first gift may have been dropping some coins into a Salvation Army bucket during the holidays or handing a dollar to a homeless person on a street corner. Because you give, you are a philanthropist.

For many, a few dollars here and there may be the extent of this giving. For others, giving may have grown into a way of life and represent thousands or even millions of dollars donated annually. But why do people give? What is their motivation for parting ways with hard-earned money?

There is always a reason or motivation for people to give, even when it seems like there isn't or shouldn't be. For the person who drops change into the Salvation Army bucket, the reason may be understanding what the Salvation Army does and enjoying making a difference through its mission. Or the reason may be emptying pockets of annoying coins jingling together. Both of these situations represent a return on investment for the donor.

So what is the qualitative difference between each of these donors and the relationship with the recipient—in this case the Salvation Army? If the motivation is to prevent a jingling pocket, then it is unlikely this motivation will inspire repeat giving or greater giving. However, if the reason is tied to the mission, then there is potential for greater investment and, consequently, greater return on investment.

I remember hearing a poem as a child that remains with me even today.

The More You Give

The more you give, the more you get
The more you do unselfishly
The more you live abundantly.
The more of everything you share,
The more you laugh, the less you fret.
The more you'll always have to spare.
The more you love, the more you'll find
That life is good and friends are kind.
For only what we give away,
Enriches us from day to day.

—Teresa Piercey-Gates

For most who read this poem, the quick conclusion is that it is about us as philanthropists. We have always been told that giving should feel good, and if we give, it will come back to us in greater measures. But imagine for a moment that the poem is really about the recipient of gifts—the nonprofit organizations on the receiving end.

Giving and receiving are not one-way streets, although that is how nonprofits and donors often perceive them. Giving of financial resources is no different than giving other kinds of gifts such as time, skills, talent, or hearts. It requires some reciprocal action to complete the act, make it satisfying, and create an experience we desire to repeat.

Most of us send holiday cards in December to nearly everyone we know. What would happen if that became our only means of interaction with those people? What if we stayed home, never called anyone, and only sent a holiday card once each year, like Peggy did in chapter 1? We would probably receive in return exactly what we invested—a holiday card.

The extent to which we invest in anything determines the return that we receive. The opposite is true as well. What we receive in return has much to do with our willingness to reinvest in the future. This is true in our jobs, our relationships, our financial investments, and our hobbies.

If golf is a passion for you, it may be because of the quality time it affords you with your friends, or perhaps the chance to be outdoors on a beautiful day, or even the mental challenge of something difficult to master. But when some choose to give up the game, they do so because the return on the investment of time and effort is no longer commensurate with the investment. Perhaps they now see golf as taking away too much time from other priorities or the frustration associated with a difficult game is greater than the joy they receive from it.

I can relate to the golf example personally. I love to play golf! But given that I travel almost every week for business, it is hard to rationalize taking five hours out of a weekend to play. I have two young children at home and a long list of honey-dos from my wife waiting for me when I walk in the door after a business trip. To make matters more challenging, I married into a golf family— meaning there are opportunities tempting me every weekend. As much as I may be tempted to take time to play golf every week, I have to weigh out the return on the investment. I need to measure playing golf against what is lost when I am away from home yet again.

We make decisions daily using this return on investment idea as the primary criteria without even realizing it. Some are major decisions like quitting smoking, perhaps because the enjoyment smoking brought us became less important than the health risks involved. Others are minor decisions like changing radio stations because we are tired of the same old songs on our regular station.

As Americans, we are raised in a culture of giving to and caring for others who are less fortunate than we are. Compassion is one of the greatest character traits of Americans. In 2012, just over $316 billion[1] was given in the United States to nonprofit organizations. No other nation comes close to these numbers. While we Americans have our flaws, generosity is not one of them.

The nonprofit sector is well aware of our generous culture. Tens of thousands of nonprofits are created each year. This continually places before generous Americans new and different ways to give time and financial resources. And the vast majority of nonprofits are well-run and worthy recipients of these gifts.

But there is a limit to which we are willing to give—and a different limit for each person. How do we choose where to invest our time and charitable giving? There are countless answers to this question because the answer is different for each individual.

Some people give to help build new buildings on a college campus for the opportunity to memorialize a family member or their love for the school. Others give to a social service agency because they see the direct impact of their gifts and the ability of the agency to serve others. Still others give out of obedience to God. In all of these circumstances, the individuals who give receive a return on their investments.

[1] Statistics according to *Giving USA 2013*

If giving, therefore, requires some return on investment to occur, it is certainly true that greater giving requires a greater return on investment.

My family and I sponsor several children in developing nations who live in deplorable conditions we cannot conceive of here. The pictures of these children adorn our refrigerator, and my own children think of our sponsored kids as their brothers and sisters. As a family, we buy Christmas gifts for our sponsored kids and, about 60 days after we send them, we get a photograph in the mail of our sponsored kids holding the gifts we sent. For about thirty bucks a month, we get a phenomenal return on our investment:

- Direct impact of our gifts through the lives of specific children

- Teaching opportunities for our own family

- Satisfaction that our money is being used for what we intended

- A connection with people who are truly in need of our help

Now, that is a great return on investment. In fact, this organization exceeds our expectations. And our response to that is we give even more to support this organization's mission. That is how it is supposed to work.

So how do we learn that? How do we figure out what motivates donors—and prompts them to give even more?

I am not suggesting that what motivates my family will motivate all people. However, everyone is motivated by something. It is the responsibility of the nonprofit organization to learn and understand what that is for their key benefactors and ultimately meet and exceed these expectations. And that is the reciprocal relationship that is foundational to a successful funding system.

Imagine a two-sided scale with the donor on one side and the nonprofit on the other. The challenge for the nonprofit is to keep the scales balanced. The greater the giving from the donor, the greater the return expected from the receiving organization. If the scales get out of balance either way, the relationship is in jeopardy. If donor expectations are under-served, then they may choose to reallocate giving to a mission that is more rewarding (provides a greater return on investment). Occasionally, the scales tip the other way, and donor expectations are simply too high for the investment being made in the mission. On these *rare* occasions, it may be prudent for the nonprofit to allow the donor to move on. Finding the right balance is the art of development.

The philosophy of the reciprocal relationship is a vital guidepost for any nonprofit that depends on charitable giving to fund its mission. Establishing this important cornerstone in a development plan will help any nonprofit organization remain focused on the most important goal of all: serving the passions and interests of its donors, so in turn, donors can serve the mission of the nonprofit.

Take a moment to reread the poem included earlier in this chapter and think like a nonprofit organization through each stanza. The more you give back to your donors as a return on their investment in your mission, the more support, loyalty, and resources you are likely to receive in return.

Chapter 3

My Definition of Stewardship

"Abundance isn't God's provision for me to live in luxury. It's his provision for me to help others live."

—Randy Alcorn

Stewardship: Now here is a word that has been used (and sometimes abused) in every application imaginable. It is used to describe everything from expressing appropriate gratitude to frugality. It is one of those words that was dubbed a "power word" a few years back and was on the same list as others like *paradigm-shift* and *robust-strategy*. It's a buzzword that sounds better than *thanks, responsibility, and stingy*—the other words we would normally use for such situations.

Many of us think of stewardship in the context of our faith. In fact, I would venture to say that most think of the term stewardship as a religious term. I think that is partly why it is so novel to use it in the business world. Taking a word out of its natural environment and using it in one where it is unexpected is a way of grabbing attention.

[2]Merriam-Webster defines stewardship this way: *The conducting, supervising, or managing of something; especially: the careful and responsible management of something entrusted to one's care.*

In the development world, stewardship often describes the way in which we maintain and nurture the relationships of loyal donors. The way we thank, recognize, and communicate with donors all fall into the category of stewardship.

Lest there be any confusion, the term **Christian stewardship** is certainly a faith-based term, yet still has as many definitions and applications as the secular version. Those who are regular churchgoers probably associate this term with giving to the church in some way. The annual church fundraising effort is usually dressed up with the word *stewardship.*

In this chapter, however, I want to offer my personal definition of stewardship—not so much as an industry term, but what it means to me and how I came to understand it in the context of the world around me. It is, for me, a word I think of in terms of my personal

---

[2] Merriam-Webster online dictionary – www.merriam-webster.com

faith journey. Rest assured, I am not going to give you my entire Christian testimony. For the sake of this chapter, just know that I am a believer and my faith impacts the way I live every aspect of my life.

Let me begin by explaining I have been a doubter and skeptic most of my life. I am one who must have a strong path of logic in order to draw a conclusion. In fact, a long and arduous decision-making process is true for nearly every strong belief I hold. If I can't back it up with sound logic, then it probably isn't something I am willing to commit to or defend. This is why I didn't become a Christian until my early 30s.

My personal stewardship journey began only about 10 years ago. The path of logic finally became clear, and I came to understand what my responsibility truly is to give freely of the resources with which I have been charged. That is not to say that I didn't give before that. I attended church and gave through the offering like most, but always with a sense of uncertainty as to whether the church and God truly needed my money.

My transformation happened back in 2004 during a trip to sub-Saharan Africa. I was traveling with a client to observe their work in the field with children who were orphaned as a result of the HIV and AIDS pandemic. We were visiting Swaziland, a small nation located near the northeast corner of South Africa. After a long journey through rough, rural roads, we arrived at a village that had been devastated by HIV and AIDS. There were hundreds of children who had lost both parents to the disease and many who carried HIV themselves, passed to them genetically. To say this was an intense experience is a gross understatement. These innocent children were suffering emotionally and physically through no fault of their own.

Sam, who worked for the nonprofit organization I was traveling with, was walking with me across a field toward a little boy who was about 7 years old, although he looked to be about 4. He was shirtless, shoeless, malnourished, and basically parentless, having been raised by an older sibling. As we approached him, he walked toward us, undoubtedly hoping we might have something for him. Ironically, he had a smile that completely contradicted everything my brain was telling me about this boy's life. He seemed to be as joy-filled as a child in any other part of the world, as if he had hope for the future.

As we neared the boy, Sam and I knelt down by him so that we were all three about the same height. Sam very casually put one of his hands on my back and the other on the boy. He then looked at me and asked a couple of questions that rocked my world.

Sam asked me about my own children at home, their ages and interests. I gave him a brief update on my three sons and daughter, while the young boy looked on, clearly not understanding a word we were saying.

Sam's next question was simply, "What do you think is really going on here?" I looked at him confused. He asked again only a bit differently, "What do you really think God is doing here?" Sam continued the questioning, "Do you think God loves your children?" I quickly answered yes. He then asked, "Do you think God loves this little boy?" I looked at the boy's face and just as quickly answered yes.

Then Sam asked one last question. "Do you believe God loves your children more than He loves this little boy?" Sam looked at me for a moment and then got up and walked away before I could even try to give an answer, leaving the little boy and me alone.

The weight of the question was just beginning to set in. My first thought was of my own children, imagining them in our home. They want for nothing and by comparison to this little boy, live a privileged life in every way. So why would God give so much to my family and me and so little to this young boy? The conclusion I reached that has subsequently changed my life is this: God had this meeting in mind and intends for those whom He blesses with much to share with those He charges with less—so that we may transform each others' lives.

In my faith journey, I have come to believe that all I am and all I have are gifts from God. I have prayed countless times for God to bless my family and to bless me with the means to provide for them. Many of us do this regularly, conceding our belief that God has at least something to do with all we are and have.

How is it that I was so fortunate to be born in a free and prosperous nation to parents who loved and provided for my every need? Why am I so privileged when so many throughout the world have almost nothing? Well, if God truly is in charge, then the only reason I can conceive is so that I will share freely and care for others.

This poem titled "Drinking from the Saucer" sums it up for me.

I've never made a fortune,
And I'll never make one now
But it really doesn't matter
'Cause I'm happy anyhow

As I go along my journey
I'm reaping better than I've sowed
I'm drinking from the saucer
'Cause my cup has overflowed

I don't have a lot of riches,
And sometimes the going's tough
But with kin and friends to love me
I think I'm rich enough

I thank God for the blessings
That His mercy has bestowed
I'm drinking from the saucer
'Cause my cup has overflowed

He gives me strength and courage
When the way grows steep and rough
I'll not ask for other blessings for

I'm already blessed enough

May we never be too busy
To help bear another's load
Then we'll all be drinking from the saucer
When our cups have overflowed

—John Paul Moore

That is my definition of stewardship and why I am moved to give. Please know that I am not sitting in judgment of others who feel differently. And make no mistake, I love nice things and do not feel guilty for my achievements and success. But I acknowledge that God is equipping me for a reason—and I cannot ignore it.

It is this clarity of stewardship in my life that is my inspiration and motivation to teach, counsel, and support leaders in other nonprofit missions. And it is the driving force behind my desire to write this book.

Take some time to consider how you have been blessed. Consider what your responsibility may be to the world around you. And then let those considerations influence your approach to fundraising.

Chapter 4

The Anatomy of a Quality Decision

"Knowing trees, I understand the meaning of patience. Knowing grass, I can appreciate persistence."

—Hal Borland

As a man who has been married twice, I can appreciate the quality of the decision involved in choosing the woman to whom I want to be married. Most of us men who have popped the question went through a long and arduous process of determining first that marriage was the right path and second that our fiancé was the right woman to marry. For those who didn't, perhaps like me, you were wiser the second time.

Being the man in a traditional relationship affords the luxury of working through this decision long before marriage is proposed.

Hopefully, the courting process also affords time for your fiancé to work through the same quality decisions. However, too often, we men know what we want and then rush our woman of choice through her decision.

I am not here to judge anyone's marriage or premarital dating process. I just want to make the point that the one who does the asking has the luxury of all the time in the world to make a quality decision. The one who is asked is frequently encouraged to hurry up and answer, lest the message be doubt and uncertainty about her proposer.

Lesson number one in life and fundraising: never try to shortcut the process for major decisions, whether you are the one asking or the one being asked.

There have been countless books written on the topic of *moves management*. (Far too many, if you ask me.) Moves management is a system intended to help a fundraiser plan and lead a donor through a decision-making process. There are no less than a hundred versions of this process published, each one pretty much as good as the rest.

Now, I am not kicking mud on moves management here. I have even created a version of my own that I teach today—although it's not in this book. Moves management can provide a helpful structure for planning, executing, and documenting the way in which we interact with donors. However, my biggest problem with moves management systems is that they usually only address the fundraiser's perspective and miss the perspective of the most important person in the equation: the one being asked.

In my opinion, before we can plan all that we want do in the year ahead with a donor, we first need to understand how the donor makes decisions. Further, we need to reach the conclusion that we are not just angling toward getting a donor to give, but rather creating an experience for the donor that will result in the highest quality of decision possible.

Put simply, I believe we first need to come at this issue from the donor's perspective. Understanding how he or she makes decisions will help us know how to most effectively use our time.

Quality decisions should be the ultimate goal of all that we attempt in major and principal gift fundraising.

There are many who work in the nonprofit sector who believe that major gift fundraising is as simple as asking donors for larger gifts. They see other nonprofits do it and therefore conclude that their own staff should be able to execute it with as much success, only without a clue of how it is actually done.

The secret to success in major and principal gift fundraising is achieving *quality decisions*. And achieving quality decisions requires a thorough understanding of the factors that must be considered when making a major decision. In this case, it is the means that justifies the end. It is not about getting to a yes, but rather, the process and the journey must be the focus.

This may sound a bit cliché because we hear this about many things in life. As kids we are always in a hurry to get to an older age and refuse to acknowledge the value of the experience in getting there. It seems like you have to get there and then look back to truly appreciate the journey. There is an art and a discipline to planning the journey that can help us all.

I feel this way about family vacations. I like to plan a family trip months ahead to allow lots of time to talk about and look forward to it. It is the months preceding the trip when, as a family, we plan the details, daydream, and put all other aspects of our lives on hold to spend uninterrupted time together that is as meaningful as the trip itself. Now, I must confess that my kids don't share the same patience and appreciation for the time leading up to the vacation, but perhaps they will someday.

There are essentially five components to a *quality decision*. They do not always happen in this sequential order, but all components are present in a high quality decision:

1. Information and Logic: the practical, head knowledge

2. Care and Emotion: the heart knowledge

3. Inspiration and Motivation: the desire to act

4. Invitation and Commitment: the stimulus and response

5. Fulfillment: the experience after the decision

Let's take a closer look at each component. In the following pages, I will define each one and then look at them in the context of a for-profit and a nonprofit example. In the for-profit example, I use the purchase of a car. Please do not leap to the conclusion that I believe fundraising is anything like selling or buying cars. This is not the case. I use this comparison because as occasional purchasers of cars, we do so cautiously and wary of car sales people. The reality is that donors sometimes are wary of fundraisers for the same reasons.

1. Information and Logic

This is the cerebral knowledge that we all seek and require to convince us that something has value. We scrutinize, list the pros and cons, and ultimately decide whether we are willing to further consider the opportunity before us.

If we are shopping for a new car, this is the work we do before we ever visit a car dealership. We usually have a general sense for the size, shape, and color we want. We probably do some research on features, reliability, and cost. If a particular car doesn't pass this initial scrutiny, then it is dismissed without much more thought or consideration.

For the nonprofit mission, information and logic is usually the primary aim of the elevator speech. Can a logical case be made for the mission that piques enough curiosity for further consideration?

If the nonprofit is a homeless shelter, then the case is easy to understand. We know why such organizations exist, and if that mission appeals to us, then we are probably willing to venture a bit deeper.

2. Care and Emotion

This is what I call the heart knowledge. Why do we care deeply about a particular nonprofit mission? It is more than mere knowledge or awareness, as it is possible to be informed about something and not care deeply about it. Take the example of one of many organizations I am solicited by every year: the American Lung Association. I understand the purpose of the American Lung Association, and I am glad they exist. I knock wood as I write this, but I don't have lung disease today nor does any member of my family. Therefore, the American Lung Association is not one of the missions I care deeply about or choose to support financially.

For the car purchase, emotional involvement comes from test driving the car and getting a taste of what it feels like. Car sales people know that if they can get you behind the wheel, you will become emotionally engaged and will be far more likely to buy the car.

Care and concern come from better understanding how a particular mission changes lives or touches our lives in some way. It is the result of someone becoming emotionally engaged in the mission.

3. Inspiration and Motivation

What motivates us to act? Again, using the car purchase analogy, the motivation may be simply a need for a new car—the lease is up or the beater finally bit the dust. Or it may be ego driven: the desire to be associated with a particular brand or style or one of countless other motivations that prompt people every day to buy a car.

There are many motivations for donors as well. We know some donors give for ego reasons, seeking public recognition or naming rights. Some want to know the direct impact of their giving on the mission they are supporting—how will their gift make a difference? We also know that some donors give out of a desire to be obedient to God and to please Him. Again, there are countless motivations that come into play, and each donor is unique. But what they all have in common is that they all receive *something* in return for their giving.

4. Invitation and Commitment

This is the stimulus or trigger that results in the action of investing or giving. For the car-buying scenario, this is the salesman asking for the sale. And if the first three components are present, then this component is expected and appropriate. If, on the other hand, the first three components are not present, then asking for the sale is awkward and uncomfortable. We have all probably experienced car sales people who are a bit too pushy and trigger-happy.

For the nonprofit organization, this step is critical to the quality of the decision. This is where the nonprofit gets the chance to assert its needs. And just like the car purchase, if everything has been done well up to this point, the invitation to commit is natural and expected.

5. Fulfillment

This is the step that is seldom done well in the automobile industry or in nonprofit fundraising. This is where the car dealership has the opportunity to truly set themselves apart from others. And this is the one area where we can all learn something from the car industry—mostly what not to do. However, there is one person in the car industry who did it right and wrote a book about it.

Carl Sewell is the Chairman of Sewell Automotive Companies, which is a collection of car dealerships throughout north Texas. He authored a book in 2002 titled *Customer for Life.* The book was about the expectations and demands of contemporary consumers, showing that businesses can remain committed to quality service by figuring out what customers want and then making sure they get it. It is about fulfillment. Any dealership can sell a car. He was committed to giving the customer a post-sale experience that ensured they would never go anywhere else with their business.

After reading this book the first time, I concluded that it might just be the best fundraising book ever written. Consequently, I have recommended it to hundreds of my fundraising colleagues and continue to use it as a reference today.

Fulfillment is what happens post-decision. The goal of fulfillment is to send the message to the investor that his or her decision to invest was the best decision he or she could have possibly made.

In the nonprofit sector, we have a tendency to go through the rote process of sending a thank-you note and other generic acknowledgements, then move on to the next donor. We too often fail to recognize the opportunity to exceed a donor's expectations.

The Art of Quality Decisions

So these are the basic building blocks to achieving high-quality decisions that consider the donor's point of view.

But there is also an art to achieving quality decisions. In other words, it is not simply about following the 10 steps outlined in the basics to fundraising textbook that lead you to the perfect result; this is another criticism I have of moves management systems. If you fancy yourself a good cook, then you have some sense for the difference between following a recipe to a T versus creating a gourmet meal. Or painting by numbers versus creating a masterpiece.

My wife, Jennifer, has taught me the difference between art and science from a musician's perspective. As a classically trained soprano, she walks through a process to learn a new piece of music that begins more scientifically and ends with pure artistry. A significant part of music is actually science and math. The intervals, time signatures, crescendos, and so on are all measurable actions that are communicated on a sheet of music. Jen will study the piece of music and begin by mechanically walking through the piece. Once she gets familiar with the mechanics of the piece, she puts the sheet music aside and begins to search for the emotion of the song—more from her heart. And that is where the beauty comes from.

As we develop relationships in our fundraising work, it may be helpful to use a moves management tool to plan and provide some structure. But developing a deep and reciprocal relationship that leads to a quality decision requires putting the moves aside and searching for the heart of it. That is the key to the most rewarding relationships and decisions that bring value to our lives.

Chapter 5

Sum of My Decisions

I shall be telling this with a sigh
Somewhere ages and ages hence:
Two roads diverged in a wood, and I—
I took the one less traveled by,
And that has made all the difference.
—Robert Frost

"The two hardest tests on the spiritual road are the patience to wait for the right moment and the courage not to be disappointed with what we encounter."

—Paulo Coelho

As I organized my thoughts for this book, I found myself dwelling on the topic of quality decisions in my life more than any other—

hence the title. I would have to say that this is the area about which I find myself getting introspective and sentimental, and it's probably the area that most underpins my personal philosophy of fundraising.

In this chapter, I offer some personal stories of decisions that helped shape my life, not because my life is more spectacular or more interesting than anyone else's. Rather, because it serves as a metaphor and foundation for my fundraising philosophy.

Also, I believe that donors' decisions to give capacity gifts can be just as defining to their lives as these decisions were to mine. When donors commit to the largest financial gift they have ever given— and perhaps even alter their lifestyle in order to make the impact they wish to make on a nonprofit mission—they choose a path at a major fork in the road.

To a large degree, we are all the sum of our decisions. I can look back over my life and point to a handful of decisions that I have made, some of high quality and some not, and see how I became the person I am today. Without question, had I made different decisions at any one of those forks in the road, my life would be very different today.

Now, all the clichés about life easily come to mind:

- Life is what we make of it.
- We control our own destiny.
- We make the bed in which we sleep.

- Stupid is as stupid does.

Clichés may sound silly, but they hold an element of truth. This is why such phrases are repeated and circulated. I can testify that these have all applied to me at different times in my life.

Regardless of the circumstances in which we live, we make decisions daily that determine the trajectory of our lives.

Let me outline a few of mine:

On Choosing a Career

I am a career fundraiser—meaning, I have been raising funds for nonprofits since the day I graduated from college, almost 30 years ago. What led me to that decision—I haven't a clue. In other words, it initially was not a quality decision. Like many new college graduates, I took my first job to make "suit money" and had no idea what I was getting into.

The quality decision came a few years later, when I had all the confidence in the world that my fundraising experience had prepared me for other, more lucrative careers. That's when I left fundraising to pursue a career in software sales. For the record, I made a fine living in this new and short career, and I am forever grateful for the time and space it gave me to rethink fundraising as a career. Yes, I ran back into the arms of fundraising after about six months in software sales! But this time, I made a quality decision.

My decision to invest my life in fundraising was based on several factors:

- **Could I make a decent living at it?** I quickly researched this issue and concluded that fundraising careers produced plenty of opportunity.

- **Did I have passion for it?** This was definitely a more difficult question because it calls for an emotional response. The answer for me was ultimately yes because: 1) I related to the missions of my clients (which seemed more significant in life than software) and 2) I loved working with the boards of nonprofits, which tend to be comprised of people who are successful in life and passionate about the nonprofit missions they serve.

- **Could I be good at it?** This answer required faith on my part, for I could not definitively answer it at that point in my career.

- **Did I want to be forever branded as a fundraiser?** I realized then that if I chose to return to fundraising, I would likely stay there for several years and then become so ingrained that it would be difficult to change careers again.

When I reentered the fundraising world, I did so with the conviction that I had made a quality decision. I was now determined to make it the right decision.

I chose to highlight this decision first because the process that led me to the conclusion is so clear in my mind. This is the decision that laid the foundation for future quality decisions and helped me reintegrate earlier decisions I had made in my youth—some of which I will now share.

Take a deep breath and hang in here with me; I promise not to pull out the home movies! But I want to share just a few brief examples of quality, and not-so-quality, decisions in my life.

On Escaping from the Delinquents

When I was 13 years old and in the seventh grade, I made a decision to turn my life around.

I lived in 14 different houses and apartments in my first 18 years of life and no one place longer than two years. Among other challenges, this meant frequent school changes. In the seventh grade alone, I attended three different junior high schools.

After going through the "new kid in school" thing two other times that year, I was not all that enthusiastic about making new friends yet a third time. So the wrong kind of relationships developed. The delinquents (aka bad eggs, thugs, future criminals) found me first and were the most eager to invite me in to their group. They were the ones who always had cigarettes and alcohol and were always willing to share. They were frequently in trouble and almost always sought to break the rules.

After a couple of months hanging with this group, I had an awakening. I couldn't really explain it at the time, but I just woke up one morning knowing I had chosen my friends poorly. I saw myself as one of the bad kids and knew I needed to change my course. I thought about it over a long weekend and decided that I wanted to be a good kid who did well in school and that hanging with the delinquents was not the way to make that happen.

I avoided the delinquents for a couple of days as a knee-jerk reaction to my new awakening. I was afraid of them—they were bigger, had no qualms with hurting other people, and would not be happy about my desire to pull away.

Because I shared most of my classes with them, I decided to go see my school counselor for help. I asked him to please rearrange my class schedule so I would not be with the delinquents all day. The counselor's solution was similar but with one disastrous difference: He attempted to solve the larger problem by changing the class schedules of all the delinquents. The delinquents were unhappy to say the least. They were furious and somehow figured out that I was responsible.

The torment began with threats and bullying in halls between classes. Although I lived less than a mile from school, I was now afraid to walk home for fear they would seize the opportunity to beat me to a pulp. So I started riding the bus. Two days later, they figured this out and were waiting for me as I got off the bus one afternoon. I didn't realize what was going on until the bus was pulling away. The chief delinquent shouted out to his two cronies to grab me. I dropped my books and started running.

Fortunate for me, I was a pretty good runner. The chase ensued in a field across the street from our apartment. I would dodge one pursuer and run for a while, then dodge another. There was one other non-delinquent kid who got off the bus with me who was watching this chase. I'm sure he thought they would catch me and that he would see a real life beating occur with his own eyes. I was running for my life and believed consequences would be much worse than a bloody nose and a few bruises. I finally yelled to the voyeur-kid to run and get my big brother.

One great benefit of having older brothers is the built-in protection factor. Having an older brother who was a bigger delinquent at the time than all of these kids put together made it even better. A few minutes later, my brother emerged with a bat in hand and made it clear that the chasing needed to stop—immediately. It did, and my brother's influence had lasting impact, bringing an end to the harassment during school. Other than a few dirty looks in the hallway, the delinquents left me alone to pursue my new path in life.

I proceeded to seek out new friendships that were consistent with my goals. The next friend I made became my best friend, and he still is to this day. He is the one who helped me find faith later in my life.

On Driving the Speed Limit

There is this unwritten rule out there that says it is okay to drive 5 to 10 miles per hour over the speed limit. Almost everyone follows this guideline and, for some reason, feels no guilt for breaking the law.

I also subscribed to this blurring of the law, even letting my speed drift up to 15 miles per hour over the limit once in a while. I received my share of citations for this. But hey, everyone does it, right?

I felt that way until I was driving my then 6-year-old daughter, Ellie, to the donut shop one Saturday morning. She was looking over my shoulder from her booster seat in the back and pointed out that I was driving 47 miles per hour (the digital speedometer was my demise). She added that the speed limit sign we were passing clearly stated that I should only be driving 40 miles per hour.

I quickly began defending myself by saying it was okay to drive a little faster because everyone did it—and then I stopped myself. I realized I was about to teach my daughter that sometimes it is okay to break the law, just because "everyone else does it." I immediately slowed down to 40 and told my daughter that she was right.

Since that fateful Saturday morning, I drive the speed limit and not one mile per hour over. Consequently, my wife won't let me drive because this makes her crazy.

On Killing an Old Lady

I once killed an 84-year-old woman. Okay, turns out I didn't really kill her, but I thought I did at the time. I was studying to be a physical therapist in college and held a part-time job at a local hospital as a transporter for the physical therapy department. That means I brought patients from their hospital rooms to the physical therapy department via wheelchair.

One Saturday morning, I entered an elderly woman's hospital room and began helping her into a wheelchair. As she was moving from the bed to the wheelchair, she let out an agonizing groan and then slumped over and turned as grey as an elephant.

I completely freaked and sprinted to the nurse station screaming for help. They came quickly and verified my story, called STAT over the intercom and brought in a crash cart to revive this poor old woman. I stood in the back of the room watching all of this happen in slow motion. She had indeed passed away, and there was no reviving her. Eventually, the nurse noticed the shock on my face and escorted me out of the room, explaining that this was not my fault.

After taking a week off of work, I came to grips with the truth that this woman's death was not my fault, but nevertheless, I resigned my job at the hospital and changed my college major to business. I knew I had no stomach for a profession that involved life and death.

I ended up landing a job at my college in the mailroom where I worked until graduation. It was there that I was first introduced to the world of fundraising. It so happened that my college was conducting a capital campaign, and there were consultants guiding the process. I interacted with them daily in the mailroom and got to know them well. When I graduated, they offered me a job, which I accepted, and I never looked back. I often thank that old lady for setting me on the right course.

On Leading an Intervention

Paul, the person who hired me for that first fundraising job, became one of my best friends in the years that followed. Paul worked very hard and was one of the best fundraising consultants I have ever known. I knew I could learn a lot from him. He was as cool as a boss could be. After a long day, he would take my associates and me out for beers. In fact, he liked to stay out *very* late and drink *a lot* of beer.

I worked for Paul for about 10 years, and we grew to be very close friends. I was married by then, with two young children at home.

He too was married with two kids. For Paul, the late nights out continued—he seemed to have no limits, regardless of his family responsibilities. I was no saint myself in those days and periodically went along with him, in spite of the trouble it caused me at home.

At some point, I began to pull back from Paul and the late nights—a deliberate decision to be a better father and husband. Paul continued to party with others, and it only increased in time. On occasion, I witnessed him taking drugs and leaving gatherings with other women. At this point, I withdrew my friendship completely, as the reality of the situation set in.

My friend had a substance abuse problem that led him to make terrible decisions. His career, marriage, and family were all crumbling away. Paul's wife discovered his infidelity one day and left him. Then Paul cancelled one too many client visits in the middle of a drinking binge and lost his job. And his car was repossessed while he was sleeping off a major hangover.

Now all this time I took the position of "to each his own." I had tried a few times to talk some sense into Paul. If this was the way he wanted to lead his life, then he would suffer the consequences.

Then the thought struck me that I might have a greater responsibility here. If I didn't help, who would?

I began researching how to conduct an intervention. A local substance abuse facility was helpful in providing the information I needed and coached me through it. I contacted Paul's ex-wife, kids, mother, siblings, and our mutual friends. We put together an army of people he loved and trusted, many from different parts of the country. The goal of assembling the intervention team, as I was instructed, was to take away any escape path for Paul.

The next challenge was getting him cornered. I was instructed by the substance abuse center to do anything it took to get Paul to spend the night at my house. I invited him to come over, watch some old movies, and drink some beer. It was the beer that got him there. He drove over in a rental car his elderly mother secured for him since his car had been repossessed. Once inside my house, a neighbor and friend disabled the engine of Paul's rental car so he had no means of leaving that night.

I served Paul beer after beer as we watched old movies and laughed together. He finally passed out about 3:00 a.m. I turned on my home's burglar alarm just to make sure he wouldn't try to escape, and then I turned in for a short night. The entire intervention team arrived at 7:00 a.m. I had gallons of coffee ready as we assembled in the kitchen. I then woke Paul from his still heavy slumber. No doubt he was still intoxicated.

He was very surprised to see all of us gathered in the kitchen, to say the least. He sat down, hair disheveled, and listened to each of us share our love, care, and concern for him. We had all pitched in to cover the admission costs at a top-rated substance abuse center. He reluctantly surrendered to us that morning and was admitted the following day.

That fateful night 16 years ago was the last time Paul consumed alcohol or drugs. He has been clean and sober since and has put his life back together. He still attends AA meetings and never fails to call every member of the intervention team each year on the anniversary of the intervention.

On Finding Faith

Those who knew me in my twenties might think I was already a believer. In reality, I was a faker and a poser—meaning I only pretended to believe for the benefit of my faith-based clients. It was actually during my time as a bachelor (between marriages) when I gave my life to Christ.

For the record, my step into faith was not a "surrender" like so many other testimonials I have heard. Rather, it was a deliberate decision based on a long intellectual battle in my brain. My decision was simply this: I choose to believe because to not believe doesn't end as well. Therefore, if I have the choice of the team I want to be on, I want to be on the one that at least has a chance of winning in the end. This has been the greatest decision of my life!

Once the decision was made, I began to read, study, worship, and think like a person of faith. My life forever changed. While there were many influences in my life, I credit my decision to follow Christ to my aforementioned friend Stuart who witnessed to me subtly through most of my teenage and young adult life.

On Choosing Partners in Crime

By any definition, I have experienced success throughout my career in fundraising. I spent my first 22 years working for two companies that gave me a great education in the industry and the environment to develop the fundraising philosophy I practice and teach today.

I left my first employer in 1990 to join a Texas-based firm that was building a new division in faith-based institutional fundraising. I climbed the corporate ladder quickly and eventually found myself in the role of president of one of three business units in the firm. Around this same time, the founder and principal of the firm decided to retire and, consequently, sell the company.

Here is where the crime begins. During the pending sale of the company, I entered a season of secret plotting with two of my colleagues. We were not thrilled with the direction the founder wanted to take the company. So the three of us, already friends, met secretly several times, pledged our allegiance to one another, and planned a coup d'état, metaphorically speaking. We would give the retiring founder an ultimatum—change the direction or lose all three of us.

Choosing to lock arms with my two partners in this crime was critical. We spent much time together and talked through all possible scenarios. We were convinced that the ultimatum would not work, but we were committed to starting a new company together. We engaged an attorney to think through non-compete issues, identified staff resources and clients we would likely pursue, and took steps to shore up seed money to start our new firm.

I'll spare you the graphic details and tell you that neither the ultimatum nor the plan to start the new company worked. Once the founder learned of our scheme, he surgically divided the three of us by offering two of us something better and cutting one loose. I was the one who drew the short straw and lost it all—so much for our allegiance.

It took a long time for me to fully recover from this emotional set back. I felt betrayed by my two partners. And although, in hindsight, choosing to partner with these two guys was a poor decision, it led to some great things, one of which was the start of my own firm.

My Ultimate Gift Some Day

Some day, I want to give a million dollars to a single nonprofit mission I care deeply about. One can deduce quickly that in order to give a million, one must have a million to give. Before the cynics jump on me for using this as a backhanded reason to become wealthy (which I am not), let me explain. In that regard, I hope I am able to give such a gift, even if it means giving nearly every thing I have.

Believe it or not, it is not so much about the amount of money I would need to amass to make such a gift. Rather, it is about two other reasons that fuel this desire within me.

The first is the impact that a million dollars will have on a mission that I care for deeply. A gift of this magnitude managed in the right way can be transformational to almost any nonprofit mission. To think that a worthy and noble mission could be transformed as a result of my decision is satisfying, and I would love to watch it happen.

The second reason is the gift I want to give my children. Not *a gift of money*, but *a message of giving and stewardship*. Not a message that I was wealthy and gave a little, but that I worked hard to earn what I did and was willing to give it all.

I have been blessed in my life with far more than I deserve. And although I have been through some financially tight times in my life, I have never been one to allow money to be a source of worry or conflict in my lift. I know it won't be as easy as I am making it out to be here, but I can already imagine the satisfaction and value I will receive in return for giving away everything I have.

Quality Decisions

The quality of our decisions means everything! Whether we are deciding on what career to pursue, if we will live a faith-filled life, or if we will give all we have for the benefit of others, our lives take the shape of these decisions. The quality of these decisions determines whether we have regrets or whether we are content.

As I have matured over the years, I can see a convergence of decisions in my life. And now, because I have a little gray hair, I think I've gained a bit of wisdom. I will leave that to you, the reader, to decide. What I can claim is that my life, faith, family, career, philanthropy, and friends seem to be in harmony. And it all stems from a few key decisions.

SECTION II

The Perfect Campaign

Chapter 6

The Challenge: An Extraordinary Opportunity

"Don't wait for extraordinary opportunities. Seize common occasions and make them great. Weak men wait for opportunities; strong men make them."
—Orison Swett Marden

Early one Wednesday morning, a pastor of a growing church awoke after a restless night of dreaming. All night long the pastor dreamed of the number *four*. He quickly glanced at the clock and noted that the time was 4:00 a.m. on the nose. As his head cleared, he realized that the date was April 4 and that Wednesday is the fourth day of the week.

The pastor had recently been wrestling with the challenge of building a new church building to accommodate his growing flock.

His church was 40 years old, and he was the fourth minister to serve in the role of pastor. He knew in his heart that the recurrence of *four* in his life was an important sign.

He reached for the TV remote on the nightstand and turned on the morning news. The TV came on to channel 4 (of course), and there was a reporter at the horse track giving a run down on the day's races, which would take place at 4:00 p.m. "That's it!!!" he exclaimed, as he dashed to the front door to retrieve the morning paper. He quickly thumbed to the sports section and then to the horseracing page (page 4). He was convinced that all of the fours in his life must be a sign that he should follow.

Sure enough, in the fourth race of the day, the fourth horse was named Quartet. He quickly grabbed the phone and called his Finance Committee Chairman. After a lengthy explanation, the pastor convinced him that placing a bet from the church reserve fund on Quartet in the fourth race to win was the right thing to do. It seemed as plain as day to him that this was how he would get the money to build the new building for his flock.

Well, you may have guessed what happened. Quartet finished fourth. No new building.

One sure thing in life is that there will always be opportunities and problems that challenge us to take extraordinary measures. It happens in our personal and business lives every day for both positive and negative reasons. It may be as frivolous as a new entertainment system that we rationalize will save us money because we will stay in and watch TV instead of going out to the movies. Perhaps it is a second location of a retail business that will bring twice the customers.

My intention is not to judge the worthiness of the opportunities or the justifications we use for choosing one over another. Rather, it is to acknowledge that we are motivated to seize extraordinary opportunities and often find ourselves perplexed with choosing the most appropriate action.

Before we proceed further down this path, let's take a moment to define an *extraordinary opportunity*:

> *An extraordinary opportunity or challenge is one that cannot be addressed through traditional means and/or resources. It requires an extraordinary plan, effort, and energy. And when complete, yields extraordinary results.*

The question to be pondered is always the same: Can the extraordinary opportunity be seized without handicapping sustainability?

We witness countless bad decisions daily as people and organizations alike take on more than they can sustain. We are all tempted to take on more of a burden in the interest of short-term gain. Regardless of whether it is an opportunity to expand our business or take on a mortgage to purchase a home, we begin by exploring what extraordinary measures can be taken to address the extraordinary opportunity.

This happens in nonprofit organizations just as often. The luminary behind every nonprofit organization at one time had a vision for an extraordinary opportunity to positively impact lives in some way through a unique mission. It is these opportunities for the impact of that mission that drives them to work every day pondering how the impact could be greater.

For the nonprofit organization with a worthy and noble mission, extraordinary opportunities frequently include building or expanding facilities to grow its programs—a mighty challenge indeed, and the questions that go along with that challenge are worthy of great consideration:

- How much will this cost?

- Where will the money come from?

- How much can we raise?

- How much can we borrow?

- How long will this take?

Quick answers often materialize with an intense focus on what this project will mean to the mission of the organization. The problem is that most of the focus and attention is on the extraordinary opportunity and not the extraordinary means to achieve it. And so, like many people, corporations, and even nations today, the nonprofit organization often commits to seize the extraordinary opportunity without a full understanding of the implications and consequences.

Now, lest I sound like a wet blanket here, I am not suggesting nonprofits should avoid planning for growth in their missions or seizing extraordinary opportunities. I am a big proponent of growing missions, aggressive planning, and risk taking. But it is the decision-making process with which I am most concerned.

Simply put, it is a fact of life that extraordinary opportunities will continue to arise before nonprofit organizations. Each one should be considered. But too often the conclusion drawn is that this may be the only opportunity and it must be seized now or lost forever. It is this conclusion that leads to quick transactional decisions that are not always in the best interest of the nonprofit.

The extraordinary measures the nonprofit will need to take in order to seize the opportunity must be considered in the context of the long-term impact they will have on the mission. And the answers are not quite so obvious—it won't be like following the signs to place a bet at the horse track. The truth is that the extraordinary actions taken to fund and seize extraordinary opportunities are just as impactful as the opportunities themselves.

Chapter 7

The Perceived Solution: A Capital Campaign

"Opportunity is missed by most people because it is dressed in overalls and looks like work."
—Thomas A. Edison

Advertising executives will attest that it's human nature to make emotional choices and then later back them up with logic and rationale. When extraordinary opportunities arise, excitement and enthusiasm are often difficult to contain. This is why we never know how badly we need a new car until we test drive one! Then we search for the logic to support what we now can't seem to live without.

Excitement and enthusiasm are good things. They are the motivations for the greatest things in life. Statements such as "How can we afford <u>not</u> to do this?" and "The money will appear because this is meant to be!" are born out of this excitement and enthusiasm. But they also must be checked against responsibility and consequences.

For the nonprofit organization contemplating a new building, the money needed to build and the emotional push to make it happen are equally important. The next step nonprofits usually take is to get two parallel tracks of activity going: one to design the new building and another devising a plan to fund it. And like parallel lines, never shall the two activity tracks meet. While the new building committee dreams of the Taj Mahal to grow and enhance the mission of the organization, the finance committee imagines that a double-wide trailer will do and can be purchased within the parameters of their current budget.

At some point, there is acknowledgement and agreement that the new building will require extraordinary measures—meaning that the cost of this project will exceed the capacity of the traditional means of funding the mission. Two options are considered:

1) We can borrow the money.

2) We can raise the money.

As these two options are discussed, the idea of doing both will surface. "If we borrow the money, we can start construction immediately," someone will suggest. "That will allow us to focus on the building and mission first and do the fundraising later to repay the loan—the best of both worlds."

Now, there are some false assumptions that have already been made that will lead to some major problems for this organization. But you can easily see how the excitement and enthusiasm can get the best of the mission-minded leadership and take them down the path outlined above.

Problem #1

Raising money to repay debt is not the same as raising money to build a new building.

Maybe you have contemplated the question, "Why do people give?" Perhaps you recall the earlier chapter titled "The Reciprocal Relationship." Perhaps you have read something else that offers some of the cliché answers to this question. It is honestly impossible to predict why people give. We all have our own unique set of motivations that cause us to give. But more broadly, we do know that people give when they see an opportunity to positively change the lives of others. We see this through support of social service organizations, churches, synagogues, educational institutions, and the thousands of other organizations we find worthy of support.

So how does this relate to funding a new building or repaying debt? When we give to fund a new building, we usually do so with an objective in mind of changing lives for good. That new building will either allow the nonprofit to serve more people or enhance its ability to serve the same people. We give because we believe that this is the only way in which the new facility will be built.

When the nonprofit decides to borrow the money to build and then raise it later in a debt reduction campaign, the entire motivation of changing lives for the good is omitted. Lives were changed back when the money was borrowed—not now when I am being asked to repay the bank. The building is no longer dependent on my decision to give.

What may appear to be a minor issue of timing to some can and will have a detrimental impact on the organization's funding plan. Look around your community today and take note of the many nonprofits that have taken this course. Many of them are now facing the tough task digging out from a mountain of debt.

Problem #2

The campaign process should have begun at least 18 months earlier if the goal was to raise the money for the new building.

This is true for any nonprofit, including the local church. It takes time to plan and conduct a capital campaign. And a capital campaign should never be fast tracked to accommodate a construction schedule. Taking steps to ensure the campaign is appropriately planned and that the passions and interests of donors are addressed should have the highest priority.

As you no doubt know by now, I earn my living by helping nonprofit organizations fund their missions through extraordinary initiatives like capital campaigns. So it shouldn't surprise you to know that I believe most nonprofits should seek out a professional firm to design and guide their campaigns. (And, of course, after seeking out several professional firms that are qualified to help, I believe that all nonprofits should engage my firm.)

All kidding aside, there are many good sound reasons to utilize professional counsel. Inevitably, the questions that cause much discussion and debate are:

1. Why can't we do this ourselves?

2. How hard can it be?

3. Wouldn't we be better stewards by keeping our costs to a minimum?

In short, the answers are:

1. No—not without serious consequences.

2. Unbelievably hard.

3. Yes, but not the way you think.

Many nonprofits have attempted capital campaigns alone, and most have regretted it. If you are part of a nonprofit that is considering conducting a campaign without professional help, please research this issue before a final decision is made. Just as you wouldn't forego the architect or build the entire staff structure with volunteers in an effort to save money, the consequences to the outcome of your capital campaign are just as great.

Campaigns are not simply about asking people for money. If they were that easy, every nonprofit could do them and there would be endless resources for their missions. Capital campaigns are complex strategic plans that encompass and engage all aspects of an organization. Having a campaign experience that exceeds the expectations of the donor base is integral to long-term relationships and credibility.

There is always a cost to fundraising and to capital campaigns. The variable is where the costs are incurred. Most nonprofits must maintain annual fundraising in order to sustain the operational funding model of the mission. Development staff members do not have the luxury of stopping their jobs for a couple of years to conduct the campaign. If this happens, not only will you have to fund development staff personnel costs from campaign proceeds, but you will also make up for the tremendous loss of operational revenue not being generated by their normal development activities.

As you can see, getting to the decision to have a capital campaign is somewhat complex. There are many forks and turns in the road, and some of those forks and turns have hidden negative consequences. Take the time to do the planning and preparation for a campaign. A poorly run effort, or one that is ill conceived, can be detrimental to the mission of a nonprofit. And conversely, a campaign that is planned and implemented well can result in the mission soaring. Funding the opportunity is hard work, but the rewards received for doing well are more than worth the effort.

When your organization is presented with an extraordinary opportunity, take time to assess the extraordinary time and resources it will require. Developing a capital campaign is a solid solution—although you'll have to free it from unrealistic expectations first. More on that feat in the pages to come.

Chapter 8

The Best Intentions:
Our Campaign Will Look Like This…

"There are many shortcuts to failure, but there are no shortcuts to true success."

—Orrin Woodward

Expectations are sometimes our worst enemy. We build them up in our enthusiasm and excitement until they reach dizzying heights.

If you have ever been through the building process of a new home, you know how quickly expectations can race out of control. In our minds, our new home will be just like the model home we walked through so many times leading up to our decision to buy. But what we find out is that the model home is full of upgrades and extras that would double the building price if we replicated it. So, with some level of dissatisfaction and disappointment, our expectations fall back to earth.

This is what often happens in the planning stages of a capital campaign. We finally commit to the capital campaign process and put our full energy behind it. But our expectation of what a perfect campaign *should* be causes the whole thing to sway and sometimes come crashing to our feet.

Here's what I've seen time and again: You have decided to conduct a capital campaign to fund an extraordinary need that is urgent and mission critical. Once the decision is made, the tendency is to begin laying down the tenets that will provide a foundation for the campaign. Great and noble ideas will be offered that, to the average board member, make perfect sense. Often, campaign utopia is described in statements like:

- *"Our campaign should only seek funding from those outside our donor constituency because our donors are already giving all they can."*

- *"We should focus more on corporations for the big money because they have so much to give."*

And my personal favorite...

- *"Let's invite everyone to give—let everyone have a stake in this new project. Our goal will be 100% participation, and we will all celebrate together when the campaign succeeds."*

Who wouldn't want that kind of campaign? This truly is campaign utopia. And if an actual campaign ever achieves even one of those ideas above, we have probably gone on to that next place where everything is as it should be.

Although these utopian notions aren't attainable in the real world, considering the pitfalls of each one is the best approach. But the key is to truly think them through! Let's do that with these assumptions.

Assumption #1: Seek New Sources

You may be wondering what's wrong with seeking funding from outside sources that haven't given before. It would be a remarkable achievement, and there are plenty of rich people out there who could fund your campaign personally with the swipe of a pen on a check.

The question that must be answered is, "Why would they?" Imagine a young man spots a beautiful woman across a crowded room and then approaches her with a marriage proposal. Is there a chance she will say yes? There is, but the odds are astronomically against him.

For a prospective donor to give a leadership gift to a nonprofit never heard of before or never supported in the past is just not likely. To cover myself, there is an astronomical chance, just like the love-at-first-sight stories depicted in romantic comedies. But the odds are that the prospective donor will not only say no, but probably will also avoid you in the future—just like the beautiful woman would avoid the seemingly preposterous young man spontaneously seeking her hand in marriage.

The solution to the young man's desire to wed the beautiful woman is to first take a risk and introduce himself, perhaps ask her to have a cup of coffee with him. Then he might pursue dating her. Assuming she agrees to the relationship, after many months (perhaps years) of doing thoughtful things, bringing her gifts, and exceeding her expectations, his marriage proposal might just be accepted.

This is also true for the prospective major donor. The lesson is the same. A nonprofit's leadership must first make a polite and friendly introduction to a prospective donor. Then leadership can take small steps toward building a trusting relationship with the donor. After many months (likely years) of communicating with the donor, doing lots of thoughtful things, and exceeding expectations, the leadership gift proposal might just be accepted.

Assumption #2: Seek Corporate Funds

Now, regarding the possibility of corporate support, perhaps one of the greatest misconceptions in the fundraising world is that corporations give away a lot of money. Before the corporate world comes out of their shoes to challenge this, let me say that there are some corporations that give generously to the nonprofit sector and set a great example for other corporations to follow. The problem is that very few actually do so.

A quick review of charitable giving trends over the past 50 years tells us that the most important and dependable source of charitable giving is individuals. That's right, people like you and me are responsible for over 70%[3] of all charitable giving in the United States. A distant second are philanthropic foundations with 15%[4] largely coming from interest earned on their asset bases. Corporate America was responsible for only 6%[5] of charitable giving in 2011, and it has never been much more than that in the past 50 years since charitable giving has been tracked.

Once again, before we leap to conclusions that Corporate America is greedy and represents the evil empire, let's consider their perspective on this. As long as I have been alive and aware, corporations have served one primary purpose: to make money. Contrary to popular belief, they do not exist to give money away.

Publicly held corporations have a responsibility to their stockholders to make money and provide return on their investments. Who among you stockholders out there is willing to forego a dividend or appreciated stock price so that the corporation can be charitable? Are we willing to allow our 401(k) to shrink because our investment portfolio decided to give away our

---

[3] Statistics according to *Giving USA 2013*
[4] Statistics according to *Giving USA 2013*
[5] Statistics according to *Giving USA 2013*

gains to build a new performing arts center or YMCA? Of course not! Your response would probably be the same as mine: "I will do my own charitable giving. You make me money, and I will decide where to give it."

Now allow me to backpedal a bit. There are some valid corporate sources for charitable giving. Some publicly held corporations choose to fund their own philanthropic foundations with a percentage of profits. Profitable corporations fund some of the largest philanthropic foundations in the United States. And privately held corporations are sometimes used as vehicles for their owners to give.

So, yes, there are *some* funds given by corporations. But remember, corporate giving in its entirety is minuscule compared to what people like you and me give. Bottom line: It is not likely that a significant percentage of your campaign funds will come from corporations.

Assumption #3: Seek Full Participation

The third statement is perhaps the most prolific in that it is the desire of nearly every organization conducting a campaign to have broad participation from the donor base. Nearly every nonprofit leader would describe the perfect campaign as one where everyone gives. But is it ever achievable, and if so, is it really a good idea?

The truth is that designing an effort to realize millions of dollars is hard. If it weren't, every nonprofit would have all the money they need. Be wary of the short cuts and the "too good to be true" ideas. You <u>can</u> be successful in funding your vision with extraordinary resources, but always maintain realistic expectations.

The best thing you can do in preparation for your organization's campaign is to release your expectations for your ideal campaign. The Perfect Campaign for your organization probably looks much different than you think.

Chapter 9

The Problem with Your 'Ideal' Campaign

"An idealist is one who, on noticing that a rose smells better than a cabbage, concludes that it will also make better soup."

—H.L Mencken

There is bit of a "people pleaser" in all of us. We humans are, by nature, consensus builders. We want people to agree with us on important issues. We look for common ground. We sometimes pretend to agree with others to avoid conflict. We frequently behave in different ways around different people in order to seem agreeable.

It is hard to run against the grain. However, we have all known someone at some point who thrives on being obstinate. If you say up, they say down. As frustrating as this may be, such a person never compromises his personal perspectives just to make others happy. It is always a question of integrity to him.

So how does this relate to capital campaigns? I believe we have a tendency to seek consensus in the nonprofit world more than anywhere else. In the corporate world, we take off the gloves because we are paid to be there and to fight for what we think is right. If someone has a differing view, they have the option of being reintroduced to broader industry (aka getting fired). It is difficult to have passionate debate among people who volunteer their time to serve a nonprofit. It is difficult to marginalize a volunteer's view or terminate a volunteer, as a means to achieving what we believe is the correct conclusion.

Before we give to something financially from our hard-earned resources, we want to believe that others will support it as well. The most frightening decision made in a capital campaign is the one made by the first donor. They wonder, "What if no one else gives to this?" We want to know that we are in good company, that others feel as we do about the projects we are funding so that those projects will ultimately be successful.

This concept manifests itself in the form of what is perceived to be the ideal campaign plan, one where everyone gives or at least one where everyone has the opportunity to give.

The rest of this chapter is dedicated to taking the unpopular path of criticizing this campaign model. I realize that, to some, this is like criticizing motherhood and apple pie. At the risk of alienating the consensus builders out there, I am committed to redefining what the ideal campaign may look like. Bear with me through the next couple of chapters, and think through the long-term interests of the nonprofit you represent. I am going against the grain, but with a noble mission in mind: to help you be more successful in your campaign endeavor. Can you believe that this comes from a big people pleaser like me? What I've learned over the years has taught me to redefine my ideal campaign to get something better than ideal—something called success.

So what's wrong with asking everyone to give to the campaign?

Simple: a little thing I call *substitutionary giving*.

Nearly every nonprofit in the United States relies on charitable giving to fund part or all of its annual operations. Private schools that garner most of their operational revenue from tuition still must have fundraising revenue to make the financial model work. Camps and retreat centers rely on fundraising to supplement user fees and guest revenue. Even the symphony in most cities must seek charitable giving to fill the gap between ticket revenue and actual expenses.

When a nonprofit organization launches a capital campaign, it must do so while maintaining fundraising for annual operations. Sometimes organizations choose not to do annual fundraising during a campaign, and that creates a whole new set of consequences and challenges. The challenge is garnering campaign funding over-and-above the current operational funding and to curtail a little something I call substitutionary giving.

Substitutionary giving occurs when a donor gives to the campaign what she usually gives to fund the ongoing and annual mission of the nonprofit.

Substitutionary giving occurs for many reasons:

1. The donor is enticed by the capital campaign solicitation process. After all, there is new and creative collateral material making a compelling case (see chapter 15 titled "The Five Most Common Challenges in the Development Office"), and they were invited to a fun reception to boot.

2. Giving to a shiny new building is more fun and exciting than giving to operations. "No one really knows what happens to operational funds.

3. The donor may not realize that giving to the capital campaign is actually different than giving to operations. After all, they still write out the check and mail it back to the nonprofit organization, same as every year.

Regardless of the reason, the fact that substitutionary giving occurs is a problem on a couple of fronts:

1. How will you address the resulting shortfall in operational funding in the immediate future?

2. How will you re-engage the donor base with the annual funding needs in the future?

This is where problems begin to pile up. Let's address the latter issue first: The development office must fight, kick, and scratch to regain the ground they lost as a result of substitutionary giving. On average, it takes two full years to climb back to where annual funding was before campaign substitutionary giving occurred.

Circling back to the first issue, too often the nonprofit board opts for a solution that seems prudent at the time but only addresses the short-term need. Perhaps they choose to allocate a small percentage of campaign proceeds back to operations to make up for the shortfall resulting from substitutionary giving—makes sense, right?

Wrong! Now a new problem arises that is far more damaging to the nonprofit. Word gets out that some of the funds raised for the new building were actually used to pay for salaries and operations, which is not what the donors intended. To some, this is a breach of integrity. Even if this was part of the plan from the beginning, there will be many who didn't read the fine print and believe there is something wrong with this decision.

In my 30 years of leading capital campaigns, I have discovered this issue in literally hundreds of nonprofit organizations. And many of those board members were not aware of it happening in the past or now. It comes from donors who gave to the previous campaign and have a memory of the nonprofit using funds for things other than what the donors intended. Trust and integrity are now in question and the potential for a successful future campaign has been partially compromised.

All right—enough already with the gloom and doom! What I want to emphasize is that the best intentions to have a great campaign seeking support from everyone only works in our imaginations. It does not work in reality. Regardless of your efforts, a minority of the donor base will actually give, and some of that will be substitutionary giving.

Rest assured that there is light at the end of this dark tunnel. It is possible to conduct a capital campaign and not impact annual funding. In fact, it is possible to address your capital needs *in addition to increasing* operational funding—all at the same time. The Perfect Campaign is the solution—and it starts in the next chapter.

Chapter 10

The Perfect Campaign in Action

"There are two kinds of perfect: The one you can never achieve, and the other, by just being yourself."

—Lauren King

The term *perfect* has been used in many contexts. I will date myself here, but I still remember Joey Heatherton in a TV commercial lying on a bed and singing to me about the Serta Perfect Sleeper mattress. Who doesn't remember George Clooney in *The Perfect Storm*—a darker use of the term, describing the ideal coming-together of nature's forces that resulted in death and destruction? Perhaps it is Nadia Comaneci's flawless performance in gymnastics during the 1976 Olympics in Montreal that makes you think of the term *perfect*. Regardless of the context, the implication is the same:

There are no flaws or impurities to take away from the focus or intent.

In terms of fundraising, what is The Perfect Campaign? Is it even possible to have such an effort? The label is a bold statement, but with good reason.

In short, The Perfect Campaign is one that achieves all of its objectives and is absent of flaws or impurities that would detract from its focus and intent. There are many campaigns that can claim part of that statement, but few that can claim it in full. Hence the term: The Perfect Campaign.

I recognize that many professional firms will make the claim that their campaign methodology and approach will not negatively impact annual funding. But the real *proof is in the pudding.* Anyone can say anything to make a sale. Therefore, we all must rely on our logic and reasoning skills to discern whether the claims people make are believable. The purpose of this chapter is not to criticize other firms or approaches. Rather, it is to make the case for mine.

So I offer the following as The Perfect Campaign.

The first factor to consider in planning the perfect campaign is: Who should be challenged to support the extraordinary opportunity? As I addressed in chapter eight, "The Best Intentions," it is neither logical nor realistic to expect support to come from sources outside of the current giving constituency. Never overlook any source for significant funding, but maintain realistic expectations related to sources for major and principal gifts.

Also addressed in chapter eight is the misconception that corporations and foundations will fund the majority of your extraordinary need. Again, always be open to rare circumstances when a corporate entity might give significantly, but don't expect it or depend on it.

That leaves the current donor base as the primary focus of the capital campaign.

The next factor to consider is: How many within the current donor base should be targeted by the campaign? This is where we begin to depart from more traditional campaign models.

To pick up on the one unanswered question from chapter eight, "Is it realistic that the entire donor base can be invited to give to the campaign?" No! Negative!! Absolutely not!!! And you shouldn't attempt it unless you have no concern about the negative impact the campaign will have on annual operational funding.

There is a certain type of donor that is ideal for funding the campaign—and what is right for one donor is not right for all donors.

Consider the analogy of a football team. When we drift off into a daydream and imagine ourselves on the Dallas Cowboys (insert your home team here) winning the big game, we see ourselves as the quarterback, wide receiver, or running back scoring the game-winning touchdown. Interestingly, we never see ourselves as an offensive lineman who ends up at the bottom of the pile during most plays.

Consider the game from the offensive lineman's perspective. He never touches the ball unless he happens to recover a fumble, which is rare. He never sees the play that we as spectators are rapt in watching. He almost always has to wait until the play is over to get up, dust off, and find out what happened.

The average fan probably can't name very many offensive linemen on teams other than his home team. Does that make the offensive linemen any less important than the running backs or receivers? If you answered yes, then consider a game without the offensive line. In fact, what if we replace the offensive line with running backs and receivers? After all, they are the players who score all the points, and it takes points to win games.

You see the absurdity in this analogy. To be sure, a team without an offensive line would be annihilated. So let's reconsider the answer to the question in the previous paragraph: Are offensive linemen any less important to the team than the running backs and receivers? Of course not! They just have to be content doing their jobs and not personally scoring the points. And the offensive line celebrates the victory every bit as much as running backs and receivers.

So let's apply this analogy to the donor base. There are only so many donors who can be allocated to providing capital campaign funds. They are the ones who will be challenged to give an extraordinary gift, over and above what they give annually in support of operations. There are only so many decisions that can be made of this caliber and quality—because it takes time and leadership to do it well. Therefore, the limited number of donors who do fund the campaign must be carefully chosen—just like the players who are chosen to catch the passes and run the ball to score the points. They are the fastest, most agile athletes the team can find.

Likewise, there is a role for many donors (most of the donor base) to play that ensures financial security for the organization in its ongoing mission. This role is much like the linemen who protect the quarterback and ensure he has the time and space to execute the game-winning plays.

And, by the way, the end of a campaign should be the same as the end of a football game. Everyone who played a role should celebrate the success.

The Perfect Campaign seeks participation from 50 to 60 sources that have the capacity to fund the entire project. This approach is predicated on the following factors:

- There are donors to every organization who have capacity to give significantly more than they are giving today or have given in the past.

- Directly addressing the passions and interests of these donors can lead to capacity giving.

- The appropriate focus on *quality decisions* will result in non-substitutionary giving.

Just in case I am in danger of losing anyone here who doesn't believe this is a realistic approach, let's look at how most traditional campaigns are funded.

Church and parish campaigns generally have the broadest participation, and even in those circumstances, less than half of the constituency participates. In nonprofits such as private schools and social service organizations, the rate of participation is significantly less.

In every campaign, a disproportionate amount of funds come from relatively few sources. For a nonprofit other than a church or parish, the top ten gifts tend to account for 60% or more of the total amount realized.

Although a traditional campaign may succeed in realizing hundreds of contributions, 95% or more of the funds realized historically come from 50 or fewer sources.

Many contributions under $2,500 tend to be substitutionary gifts, normally given to support annual operations.

Statistically speaking, regardless of the intentions of garnering broad support, campaigns for most nonprofit organizations seldom succeed in engaging the majority of the donor base. Ironically, it is the intent and effort to secure broad participation that creates problems for the organization in the form of substitutionary giving.

The Perfect Campaign simply acknowledges the reality of capital campaigns and channels all effort and energy into making this model as successful as it can be. It does so by bringing more focus to the following:

- Identifying 50 to 60 donors who have the capacity to fund the extraordinary opportunity

- Creating the steps and strategies for engaging these prospective donors in the planning process

- Gathering as much anecdotal information around prospective donors' passions and interests as possible

- Crafting a deliberate plan to directly address their passions and interests

- Allowing development staff and most current donors to remain focused on funding the annual operations of the organization

It is this last item that ensures the campaign is truly successful and can remain focused on the extraordinary opportunities to grow the mission.

So when someone espouses the ideal campaign as one that is funded by outside sources, funded by corporations and foundations, or funded by all current donors, consider this novel idea: Let's get the campaign funded by those who have capacity and interest in funding it. While we are doing that, let's also try to get all of those outside sources, corporations, and remaining current donors to help us address our annual funding needs—the life blood to sustaining the mission.

The next chapter will take us deeper into the philosophy behind The Perfect Campaign.

Chapter 11

The Wealth of Your Existing Resources

"The three great essentials to achieve anything worthwhile are, first, hard work; second, stick-to-itiveness; third, common sense."

—Thomas A. Edison

Discouragement is an active enemy to success in life. We may start off on a new venture with enthusiasm and excitement. But as the work, diligence, and mindset required to see it through becomes clear, it's easy to lose heart and take shortcuts.

We have all begun new hobbies only to toss them aside after realizing the difficulty in doing them well. I have been playing guitar since the age of eight and still enjoy strumming my acoustic at home on occasion. Each of my four children at one time or another expressed interest in learning to play the guitar. Their interest quickly waned as they realized you couldn't simply pick up a guitar one time and make music. It actually required hard work, practice, and patience.

It is one thing to *decide* to do a campaign the way I described in chapter ten. It is quite another to *just do it*. Campaign development takes an enormous amount of dedication and planning. If it were easy to go out and get 50 gifts that total $6 million, everyone would do it, and I would be out of a job. The key to success is understanding and buying into the philosophy behind the plan.

It is a common misnomer for nonprofit leadership to see major gifts fundraising as simply asking for larger amounts. It is relatively easy to ask for and get a $1,000 gift. But it is a considerable challenge to ask for and receive a $1 million gift. So let's examine this idea from few different angles.

First consider the potential donor's perspective. How might the decision-making process be different for a gift of $1 million versus that of $1,000?

Consider the banker who loans money for a living. We all know how easy it is to get a credit card. Banks will give them to anyone— even college students who are not employed. But try to get a small business loan for $1 million and see how the decision-making process of the banker changes. They want to see the business plan, budgets, payroll records, and invoicing, and then stake claims on your firstborn child.

Instinctively, a prospective donor's decision changes in a similar way. Most people will give a $1,000 gift with very few expectations. They are not overly concerned how the money will be spent and probably do not expect much more than a sincere thank-you note from the organization's CEO.

The same donor's consideration of a $1 million gift is probably much different. Let's call this prospective donor Veronica. Veronica will most likely want to understand in some detail how her gift will be utilized. She may request the business plan for the organization to give her confidence in how the investment will be used. She may want to know the specific impact of her gift. And it's even possible that she may ask for a sign to be hung over the front door that says, "The Veronica Center."

Let me offer one more example that will take the focus off of a million bucks and show the relative nature of this challenge. Most of us have at one time or another walked past a homeless person (let's say a man for this illustration) and stopped to give him $5 with the intent of providing him with a hot meal. We offer that gift to the homeless man expecting almost nothing in return— meaning, we don't expect him to report back to us on the use of the five bucks.

Likewise, many of us have attended a charity event, and after the invitation was made from the podium, we have given a $500, $1,000, or larger gift. Other than a thank-you note, we expect little or nothing in the way of reporting for this gift. We trust that the nonprofit will use this gift responsibly and where it is most needed.

So why wouldn't we give the $1,000 gift to the homeless man? There is no question that he needs it. If the man asked for $1,000, we would probably chuckle and give him the $5 we were planning to give. Suddenly, with the increase in gift value, we are faced with a different kind of decision with new considerations.

Most of us would agree that giving a thousand bucks to a homeless man carries great consequences. We may inadvertently be putting him in danger with that kind of cash. There are others on the street that might roll him in an alley for a fraction of that amount. We are not sure the man would use it for the right things. He could do more damage to his life than good if the funds were used in a destructive way. But if those concerns could be addressed, would that change things?

Maybe.

One more twist. What if the homeless man presented you with a well-thought-out proposal, showing you how he would transform his life with a gift of $1,000? What if he laid out a 90-day timeline and projections for how the money would be used? What if he promised to report back to you each week keeping you apprised of his progress? And what if you could give it to him in small installments over the 90 days, contingent on his plan being implemented? Some of us would probably give him the $1,000 under these conditions.

The point here is not the amount of money involved. It is more than that. It is the amount of money relative to the recipient. The relationship between the donor and the recipient drives the manner in which the decision is made. A prospective donor's decision to give $1 million almost always comes as a result of careful consideration of many factors and with great discernment. In most cases, the decision will also take much longer than a small gift decision. It is this very decision-making process that should drive your campaign strategy.

The primary objective of the perfect campaign is to achieve 50 to 60 exceptionally high-quality decisions. It is the quality of the decision that leads the donor to give a new and non-substitutionary gift. A deeper explanation is provided earlier in chapter four, titled "The Anatomy of a Quality Decision."

As a reminder, a Quality Decision consists of five components:

1. Logical understanding: This is the head knowledge that is necessary for initial interest in a project. A logical understanding of the proposed extraordinary opportunity (the case) is foundational to a prospective donor going deeper into the decision-making process.

2. Deep sense of care and concern: I also call this "heart knowledge" or the emotional attachment that must be part of a donor's decision to consider a capacity gift. It is possible to be informed about something without having great care or

concern. That is the difference between a transactional financial gift and a transformational legacy gift.

3. Inspiration to give: Why does a particular donor give? Everyone gives for some reason, and it is different for every donor. Discovering the specific motivations for an individual and then providing opportunities that speak to his/her motivations is integral to achieving a capacity gift.

4. A specific invitation to give: A deliberate and personalized invitation to give a specific gift to the campaign is necessary to helping the prospective donor understand the nonprofit's needs.

5. Fulfillment after the gift: Helping the donor realize that giving this gift was the best decision he or she could have made. And, if done successfully, a gift they would consider giving again in the future.

The most frequent mistake that traditional campaigns make is focusing on a process that only includes the first and fourth components. And the result is that the campaign raises some money but comes nowhere near achieving capacity giving or addressing the campaign's complete financial needs.

So now let's flip things back around to look at it from the nonprofit's perspective. What can the nonprofit organization do to proactively guide a prospective donor through a *quality decision*? The short answer is, invest heavily into building a deep relationship.

The long answer will be different for every prospective donor. The rule to remember is the one that was presented in the chapter titled "The Reciprocal Relationship": *every action has an equal and opposite reaction*. It is the reciprocal nature of a relationship that makes it work. The more time, effort, and energy you invest in donor relationships, the greater the return on those investments will be. It cannot and should not be rushed. If it is rushed, the prospective donor perceives that this really is only about money.

We often hear the expression, "It's a marathon, not a sprint," used to describe the importance of pacing. If any of you readers are marathon runners, you know the importance of making a race plan and sticking to it. When the marathon begins, everyone is excited. Most have spent months in training and preparation for this moment, and it all comes down to that shot from the starting gun. Adrenaline is pumping through your veins as the crowd at the starting line begins to move forward. The moment you see a break in the crowd, you have the urge to bolt ahead. Running seems easier than it did during the training runs, and after a short time, you check your watch. You suddenly realize that you are running at a pace that is considerably faster than the pace at which you trained. What to do?

Slow down and pay attention to what got you there! Don't squander your energy to satisfy the urge to run ahead or keep up with the other runners. Let the others run ahead. You will pass them later when they are walking because they did not remember the plan they made and the training that got them there.

The real lesson in the marathon analogy is to be wise—don't succumb to your desire for short-term gratification.

It is a well-run development operation that ensures the budget is balanced and that there is sufficient time to consider the donor's perspective. There is no fixed amount of time that a donor needs to reach a quality decision—it is different for each one. To give into the urge or temptation to take shortcuts with donors for the sake of addressing the short-term need will only result in regret later.

Launching a capital campaign is not for the faint of heart. It takes much planning, preparation, and diligence to see it through to success. The stepping-stones provided in this chapter and all of Section 2 outline the path to seeing your campaign reach its greatest potential. Section 3 details other factors necessary for making the most of your capital efforts.

SECTION III

Cornerstones of Success

Chapter 12

The Two Customers of Every Nonprofit

"If it weren't for all of these high maintenance donors, we could get a lot of work done here."
—Some nonprofit program staff

Perception is everything. It's the filter we use to assess circumstances, work, relationships, and more. A faulty filter causes us to arrive at a faulty or skewed assessment. Our perception defines us, for good or for ill.

Perception is key in development too. It determines our assessment of two critical questions that nonprofits must answer: What is your job, and who is your customer? Most organizations get them wrong. I suppose to be more accurate I should say that the answers commonly given are only partly correct; they are often introspective and sometimes even include all or part of the organization's mission statement.

So how about it? What is your job and who is the customer of the nonprofit mission you represent?

Let's imagine for a moment that you are a gourmet chef or a painter. It may seem easy to identify who the customer is—the buyer, right? But your job is to produce works of art, either in the form of gourmet meals or paintings. Do you cook or paint to please the potential customer, or do you create to please your inner artist? Ideally the answer is both, but there are plenty of artists out there who believe that integrity is compromised if you create to please the buyer.

This purist mentality works beautifully if your creations turn out to be appealing to potential buyers. But if they don't, then you either starve or you must adjust your philosophy to accommodate the buyers' interests.

I have seen this same scenario play out in many nonprofit organizations. If the vision of a nonprofit is to serve those who are the primary focus of its mission, then everything is likely designed and built with that particular customer in mind. Seems right, right?

It is right only if the vision is also appealing to those who will potentially fund it—*the other customer*. If the vision does not motivate the other customer to support the mission, then the vision is not funded or the vision must be adjusted to accommodate the funder's perspective.

Let's look more closely at the nonprofit mission of a private school as an example. If we walk into the school and ask the first person we see—probably the receptionist—to tell us who the customer is, we can guess the answer: the student! Of course! That is why the school exists: to provide a private educational experience for students that's different from and likely more specialized than what's offered by the local public school system.

If we continue on our tour through the school to ask the faculty this same question, they will undoubtedly offer a similar answer, probably dressed up in some academic vernacular. Next, we find the principal of the school, who gives us the most well rehearsed answer so far. After all, principals are saying this stuff every day, and it just rolls off their tongues. Their answer may even include the students' families, because the principal is the one who must deal with high maintenance parents as challenges arise. In reality, if we spoke with each person in the school, we would get some variation of this answer as they describe how their jobs relate uniquely to the students.

So what is wrong with this answer we received? It is correct in that the school exists to serve the educational needs of the students and their families. Someone had a vision for an educational experience and mission and then acted on that vision to create the school that exists today.

The same could be said for any nonprofit mission. A homeless shelter's customers are the men, women, and children who are in need of shelter and food.

These answers are not incorrect. But neither are they fully correct. Something key is missing.

And the missing answer may have come to mind given that this is a book about fundraising from the donor's eye view. That's what's missing. What about the donor? Yes, the donor is the other customer in every nonprofit mission and is almost always different than the first customer. Even in the private school scenario where one may think that tuition revenue pays all the bills, fundraising is still necessary to make the financial model work.

The "dual customer" is one of the most important differences between the for-profit and nonprofit worlds. In the for-profit world, this dual customer scenario rarely exists. In other words, the person with the money to invest in the product or service is usually the same person who receives the value of the product or service. Not so in the nonprofit world—at least not in the same form.

Every nonprofit has two different sets of customers. The first set, appropriately so, is embodied in the target of the mission (the student, the homeless man, the starving child). The second set, is equally important—these customers are the donors who fund the mission. Neither customer can exist without the other. Donors must have passion for a mission—and a mission must have funding, or the first customers will not be served.

So who is it within a nonprofit mission that thinks about the needs of the other customer—the donor? Let's go back to our tour of the private school. Everyone with whom we have spoken so far (receptionist, faculty member, and principal) would likely give us the same answer: "Oh, that would be the development director. Her office is down the hall on the right."

Once again, only a partially correct answer, and I am not referring to the location of the development office.

So why does everyone identify with the target of the mission (the student in the case of a school) but only the development staff identifies with the donor? I admit that I am speaking in absolutes here and that many organizations are not this blind to the existence of the donor as a customer. But I have found this is reality to some degree in most nonprofits. And the great irony is that **ALL** nonprofits want and need more funding. Further, I am willing to bet that there is absolutely no mention of the donor in the organization's mission statement.

A critical and foundational objective for any growing and thriving development operation is to know who the customers are. Everyone has a role in acknowledging the donor as a vital and equal customer to the organization. That doesn't mean that everyone has to ask for money. It just means that everyone should be aware that the donors are customers and carry some responsibility for providing good customer service.

In the school example, this means that all school faculty and staff should at least be aware of why the development office exists and of the events and activities that raise money to supplement tuition and fund the mission of the school. The reality is that faculty members are afforded far greater access to parents than the development office will ever have. If a parent is seated next to her son's math teacher during a school basketball game and asks why the school has to raise money given the current rate of tuition, the teacher should have the correct answer.

Please don't let the private school example lead you to believe this scenario does not apply to all nonprofits. Fundraising is even more critical in other organizations because most nonprofits do not have the luxury of tuition revenue.

So here are a couple of thoughts for all nonprofit leaders (staff and board alike) to ponder in the pursuit of funding growth—and all nonprofit leaders desire funding growth.

1. Change the understanding and culture of fundraising among all of your staff. While there is likely a development office down the hall, and they have primary responsibility for raising the funds, help everyone understand that they are part of the development team and have some responsibility for supporting all development efforts.

2. Craft a second and complimentary mission statement that addresses the second and equally important customer: the donor. This will help staff, leadership, and volunteers

understand the importance of the donor to the success of the mission.

It is vital to acknowledge the importance of the donor to the success of any nonprofit mission. Everyone associated with a nonprofit must also be part of the development team. Not necessarily as front-line fundraisers, but at least in roles of support and spirit. Remember, it is the magic of bringing the two customers together that transforms lives. How you answer the two critical questions will make or break your capital funding goals.

Chapter 13

The Key to Successful Volunteer Leadership

"No great manager or leader ever fell from heaven; it's learned not inherited."

—Tom Northup

I grew up in the western suburbs of St. Louis, Missouri – a fairly parochial community that the rest of my family and most of my friends never left. We were a typical lower middle class family who rarely traveled outside the Midwest. During my childhood, I lived vicariously through the eyes of my friends who traveled to other parts of the country I had not seen. I specifically remember as a young boy hearing one such friend describe New York City as a place full of rude people.

My friend's impression of *rudeness* was the result his encountering one rude person on the streets of New York City. That coupled with hearing an unfamiliar east-coast accent from most he encountered, observing the speed with which New Yorkers move, and their lack of interest in making small talk with tourists brought him to the conclusion that "all New Yorkers are rude."

As a product of a parochial environment, my friend's opinion became my own, which I shared with conviction with anyone who would listen. What a mistake I had made by accepting a stereotype without any firsthand observation or evidence.

Stereotypes develop because a pattern is found and then liberally applied to anyone and everyone within arm's length. In the nonprofit realm, one such stereotype is about the unreliability of the volunteers.

I can't begin to tell you how many times I hear from executive directors of nonprofit organizations that volunteer leadership is unreliable. This is usually based on some previous experience they have had trying to put a major responsibility into the hands of a volunteer and then watching it fail. Although stereotypes don't materialize out of thin air, the good news is that it's possible to demolish that stereotype with the right approach.

In my experience, the problem is not necessarily with the volunteer leader, but more so with the way in which the volunteer leader was engaged.

If one's experience managing personnel is only in the for-profit sector, then one might expect there to be some struggle managing and supporting volunteers. The difference seems obvious but isn't always addressed in practice. The bottom line is that you must motivate volunteers from multiple perspectives and differently than paid employees.

When I need some help from my oldest son, Schuyler Jr. (now grown and independent), to do something too physically strenuous for me to do alone, I have to motivate him to help. I no longer have the leverage of punishment or withholding allowance to coerce him into doing things he doesn't like to do. I now have to entice him with something he will enjoy. So, for Schuyler, motivation can be found in an evening by the grill with some music or a father-son outing at the driving range.

Likewise, I have found proper motivation with volunteer leadership to be extremely effective in nonprofit fundraising and integral to the success of any extraordinary effort. In fact, of all the contributing factors to a successful campaign, I believe volunteer leadership is the most critical. Campaigns are not really won or lost in the later stages like we might think. They are won or lost before they even get started, when we are engaging leadership, establishing precedent, and setting expectations.

There are three critical components to engaging effective volunteer leadership:

1. **Identification**

2. **Enlistment**

3. **Orientation**

1. Leadership Identification

Too many nonprofits that are preparing to enlist a campaign or event chairperson begin by discounting those they think are too busy or will decline for other reasons. Huge mistake!

The first rule when identifying candidates for any key leadership position is to consider the "dream team" leaders, regardless of how we think they might respond. How to get them to say yes is a different challenge entirely.

The next rule is to make sure you are considering the right leadership characteristics for the job. Consider again the campaign chair position. You are looking for the person who can help you raise the most money, not the person who has been around the longest or is the most active and beloved volunteer leader.

As we analogized in a previous chapter, if you are looking for a quarterback for your football team, you wouldn't only consider those who have the time to play. Rather, you would consider those who have the talent to lead you to victory. The role of a campaign chair is just as important.

Some common selection errors include:

- **Selecting a campaign chair who pre-emptively steps up and volunteers.** It would be an amazing coincidence if that person turned out to be the best possible leader for the campaign.

- **Picking someone because he or she has the time.** "We should look for a retired person who does not have a career that will conflict with the campaign." I have found that people who have the time are not nearly as effective as busy people.

- **Selecting someone from the board whom you want to see become more active.** The campaign is not for experimental leadership.

- **Keeping the chair of the building design committee as a carryover.** In this case, continuity is not your friend.

- **Picking someone because they have done it before somewhere else.** It cannot be the responsibility of the chair to develop the fundraising plan, so don't pick someone on the basis of having that skill.

If the role of the chair is to give you the greatest chance for fundraising success, then she/he must be someone who can lead by example throughout the campaign in every way:

- **Giving.** The chair must be someone who is capable of giving one of the largest gifts to the campaign. This characteristic is important because the chair needs to be able to challenge her/his peers to consider similar gifts.

- **Asking.** If the chair is unwilling to ask and challenge others to give, the campaign is doomed from the start. The attitude and actions of the chair will largely determine the actions of other volunteer leaders enlisted later in the effort.

- **Advocating.** With integrity, conviction, and confidence, the chair must believe in the mission and objectives of the campaign. This is critical to the campaign's credibility. If the chair is someone the broader constituency holds in high regard, then the campaign benefits immensely from her/his advocacy.

2. Leadership Enlistment

The manner in which a volunteer leader is enlisted has as much to do with success as the identification process. The invitation to serve in a key leadership role should send the message of importance. Getting the right candidate to say yes to the role of chair is similar and should be taken as seriously as securing the campaign's top gift.

This is one of the most common areas where I see mistakes made by organizations electing to conduct their campaign without professional counsel. It is never as simple as it seems to put together a campaign leadership team, and it is next to impossible to undo a mistake once it is made. If a leader is not enlisted correctly, "the horses have left the barn," and there is little that even a professional firm can do to fix the problem.

Some common enlistment errors include:

- **I know Elizabeth very well and can enlist her with a phone call.** One of the worst possible ways you can take a potential leader for granted.

- **Describing how easy the job will be.** This would be a bald-faced lie.

- **Assuming you don't need a leadership proposal and well-thought-out enlistment plan.** Again, taking the prospect for granted and lessening the importance of the role.

The general rule of thumb to guide enlistment is: *Never take anything for granted.* Assume that you need to go to the greatest lengths possible to garner a yes response to the invitation to serve. Even though sometimes the familiarity and friendship with a leadership candidate may make you think you can enlist more informally, you end up sending the wrong message—that the campaign and the role you are attempting to fill are not all that important.

3. Leadership Orientation

If you have followed my counsel on the first two components, you have gone to great lengths to set precedent with the identification and enlistment process. And, it is just as important to continue setting precedent through the orientation of the newly enlisted leaders. That means you must know and communicate exactly what you desire and expect from each one.

One of the most common reasons why it is so difficult to get volunteers to say yes to a specific leadership role is that they do not instinctively know how to carry out the responsibilities for which they are being enlisted. Even as part of the enlistment process, it is important to help prospective leaders understand you don't expect them to figure out how to do the campaign by themselves. They must be assured of three things: 1) there is a sound plan in place, 2) his/her role in that plan is well defined, and 3) there is adequate support in place to help them be successful.

Some common orientation errors include:

- **How hard can a campaign like this be? We will figure it out together as we go.** If I am the leader and this is the message, I would sneak away in the night and never return.

- **The reason we invited you to this role is because we know you did this once before for the YMCA.** Oops! Again, a reason to flee. This may be the most important reason to have professional counsel on board.

The message here is simple: The chair needs to be enlisted into a plan that can and will succeed. If the plan is not yet developed, then the message you send is, "We really don't know what we are doing. Can you figure this out for us?"

As I stated in the opening paragraph of this chapter, the selection, enlistment, and training of volunteer leadership for any campaign or annual fund are the most critical variables. When campaigns fail, ineffective volunteer leadership is usually the reason. But it is not necessarily their fault! Sound confusing?

Imagine you had the task of enlisting a volunteer army to wage a war against some aggressive bad guys. If you casually recruit your force, down playing the role and responsibility they will have, then expect them to create their own battle plan and training regiment, and wait for them to be crushed by the opposition. Most would not agree to serve on such a force, acknowledging the slim chance for success.

Instead, if winning is the only option, you would likely begin with a professional advisor who has been victorious in battle many times before to help you craft a plan. Next, you would enlist a credible leader whom others will follow with confidence. Then you would surround that leader with well-trained lieutenants and troops.

Through the entire enlistment process, you would do your best to set the precedence of professionalism, priority, and confidence in victory.

The point here is that winning the campaign for a nonprofit is critical: There are grave consequences to failing in such an effort. The people you enlist into volunteer leadership positions are the ones who must ultimately own its success. The way you identify, enlist, and train them has everything to do with how they will perform. Putting people who are not trained and supported into leadership roles that are not well defined is a recipe for failure.

Set your volunteer leaders up for success. Say goodbye to unreliable volunteers with an approach that breaks the mold.

Chapter 14

The Role of Board Leadership

"We are not a fundraising board!"
    —Far too many nonprofit board members

All too often I hear the statement in the opening quote from board members, suggesting that they didn't sign up for any fundraising responsibilities. "We are an advisory board (or policy board, or governing board, or fill-in-the-blank board) . . . anything but a fundraising board.

Does that sound familiar?

Before I go too much further here, let me say that I am not trying to throw board members under the bus for not being crazy about fundraising. In fact, no normal person is crazy about fundraising— its popularity is somewhere between root canals and colonoscopies on most people's list of favorite things to do. In addition, board members are volunteers who are busy people and have only so much time, effort, and money to give in support of a nonprofit mission.

So what exactly do most board members believe their roles to be? And what should the role of a board be to most effectively advance the mission of the organization?

The answer to the first question is fairly easy. Most board members understand their roles to be what is defined in a job description that they don't remember reading. It is somewhere in the board binder with all of the by-laws of the organization. Therefore, if asked, few board members would give matching answers to this question.

Like many who read this book, I am a parent. I have four great kids who have enriched my life in ways I can't begin to describe. As a father, I play many roles in the lives of my children. I am a provider, a teacher, a mentor, a playmate, and much more.

When my youngest son Jack comes home from school, he often asks me to play with him. Imagine that Jack asks me to play catch with him in the backyard, but I proceed to explain to him that I am not really a *playmate* kind of dad. "I am really more of a provider kind of father."

Jack would look at me like I was from another planet, and he would be right. He would be thinking, "You are the only dad I have. Who is supposed to teach me how to throw and catch?"

Now consider the relationship of a board to its nonprofit organization. It is similar to that of a parent and child in many ways. A board provides discipline, accountability, guidance, support, tough love, and more.

I believe the question to ponder is: What role <u>could</u> a board have? Not, what role has it had in the past? Or, what role does our job description outline?

Unless you are one of those board members who seeks only to add something to your resume, you probably genuinely care about the mission you represent. And it's crucial for you to remember, how my son Jack might have felt in the illustration above: You are a member of the only board the organization has. If you are not willing to help, then who will?

For any nonprofit with a healthy and growing fundraising operation, the board is an integral ingredient. Not just giving, although that is an important part, but also in the way they engage their personal networks of friends and acquaintances, the way they advocate the mission of the organization to people they meet, and the way they give of their time and skill set. If a board member— one of the foremost volunteer leaders of the organization—is not willing to do these things, then why should someone who is not as engaged with mission?

The most important role a board member can play is that of "leader by example." Board members must demonstrate the way they want others to get involved through giving, advocating, and volunteering.

It is one thing to sit here in my role as counsel to a nonprofit and lecture board members on what they should be doing, and it's quite another to dive in and get my own hands dirty. Let me assure you, I recognize that it is much harder to do these things than to instruct others to do it.

As I have served on boards and had to actually put my time, skills, and resources where my mouth is, I have rationalized it this way:

I choose to serve on this board because I believe in and have passion for its mission. If I don't believe, then I should get off the board and let someone else who does believe step into the role.

As a passionate supporter of this mission, my life has been enriched by becoming more deeply involved through giving and volunteering. If the mission enriches my life, it stands to reason that it may also enrich the lives of my friends. I therefore feel comfortable introducing and recommending this mission to my friends on that basis—much the same as I might recommend a good book, movie, or restaurant for the same reasons.

Some will choose to support it because they believe as I do. Others will choose not to because they do not experience the same life enrichment.

If you are in a position to guide or facilitate a session with your board, consider utilizing the analogy of the board as a parent, and then ask the board members to consider the many ways they could nurture, support, guide, and grow the mission. When unencumbered by a job description and left to consider the meaning of leadership, the sky is the limit.

Whatever role your board has played in the past, it's time for you to leverage those limited slots with leaders who believe in the mission of your organization. Your capital development will be maximized—or minimized—based on the strength of your board. Set your capital campaign on a course for optimal success with a board that leads the way.

Chapter 15

The Five Most Common Challenges
in the Development Office

"Good judgment comes from experience, and experience comes from bad judgment."

—Rita Mae Brown

Wisdom in life comes from having lived through and experienced adversity. We all want to have wisdom long before we attain it. As parents, we know we have to let our children make mistakes in order for them to truly learn. There is no shortcut to becoming wise.

In my travels and time with hundreds of development directors, I never stop learning new and good ideas that are being successfully implemented. I am not under the illusion that I know everything—I only know what I have learned from my colleagues over the past 30 years. Therefore, the content of this chapter is one of sharing the ideas discovered by many colleagues and, perhaps, identifying some trends that flow from this insight.

Every nonprofit organization is different and has its unique challenges and circumstances. There is good work being done today in most development offices.

But there are a few challenges that plague the funding operation of most nonprofits. Here are the top 5 I've noted:

Challenge #1: A Weak Case for Giving

"The biggest problem with communication is the illusion that it has been achieved."

—Robert Stevenson

A common challenge I see in the nonprofit world is that every organization believes they have the most compelling mission. While it is good to have passion for and confidence in your mission, believing that it is compelling does not make it so.

When my son Trevor was 5 years old, we put him on his first soccer team through the YMCA. He was a happy kid and thrilled to be on a team. He had neither a clue of how to play soccer nor the desire to learn—yet he believed he was one of the fastest and best players out there. The only contact he actually made with the ball was accidental; the chances of him scoring a goal were similar to my odds of winning the lottery. His belief that he was great was good for his self-esteem, but it did not make him a great soccer player.

There is potentially a compelling case in every nonprofit mission, like there is potentially a good soccer player in most children who are learning the sport. The difference is that nonprofit missions don't have the luxury of a long learning curve.

What makes a case compelling? There have been many answers offered to this question, but few good ones. I offer this for your consideration: *A compelling case is one that shows how lives are changed for good.*

It is easy to take your mission for granted, especially if you live deep within it every day. Seeing the forest for the trees can be a challenge indeed. We sometimes think that donors understand our mission as we do and forget that we need to show them specifically how it works.

The key is that most donors want to understand the impact their giving makes on your mission. Assuming your mission affects people's lives in some qualitative way, your case must convey the measureable impact. This should take the form of functional data that appeals to the left-brain coupled with real-life stories that appeal to the more emotional right brain.

To achieve the right and left brain goals requires collateral that is current and brings your mission to life—more than an annual report or direct mail letter. It requires a fresh perspective produced in a creative form, a staff well trained in giving the elevator speech, and time in front of donors to open a dialogue.

Challenge #2: Too Many Events

"Let's try to raise money without letting the donor know they are actually giving."
—The mastermind behind most events

How many events do you currently conduct each year? If the answer is more than two, then you are likely wasting staff time and money and limiting your potential for growth.

Most development offices that have been in existence for a while reach this conclusion without any help. The problem is that once events are started and work their way into the calendar and culture of a nonprofit organization, it is next to impossible to stop doing them. They become *sacred cows* to the board and volunteers.

I recognize that this issue applies to the vast majority of small- and medium-sized nonprofits out there, and there are likely some who are reading this section ready to take up arms defending their events. So let me say right here and now that there are some good things that can be accomplished by conducting a special event. But events also have some bad and ugly to consider. Let's look at all three.

The Good of Events

- **They are fun.** They provide an opportunity to bring donors together, blow off some steam, and build relationship networks.

- **They identify new donors.** An objective of every event should be to bring new friends and donors to the organization—assuming you can capture their information for future contact.

- **They can deepen the relationships with existing donors.** If designed and executed properly, an event can be an excellent mid-level donor strategy.

The Bad of Events

- **Most events are not mission focused.** They entice people to give to something (a golf ticket, an auction item, etc.) other than to the mission.

- **They give development staff a false sense of accomplishment.** Because events require so much time and attention from staff and volunteers, it's easy to mistake being busy for being effective.

- **Events do not challenge donors to give anywhere near their capacity.** The premise of most events is to passively raise money by not really asking.

The Ugly of Events

- **Most events are grossly inefficient.** The truth is they don't raise enough money relative to their cost. And when actual staff costs are factored in, many events actually lose money.

- **They monopolize resources.** Event planning takes significant chunks of staff time that could otherwise be utilized in more efficient and effective fundraising activities.

The long and short of special event fundraising is that there is a place for them in every development operation—but in moderation. Most development operations are out of balance and continue making this mistake year after year.

Challenge #3: Too Inwardly Focused

Development staff can sometimes get so wrapped up in managing the budget and expectations of leadership and the board that they forget what they are supposed to be doing.

When I was in high school, I worked in a grocery store stocking the shelves. My job was to keep the shelves looking full and make sure there was plenty of everything to accommodate the flow of shoppers. Around any major holiday, the grocery store would get so busy that I would have to help check out customers at a cash register. The line of customers at times seemed to never end. Meanwhile, the shelves were becoming empty because I was not able to keep them stocked while working the cash register. I remember saying to myself, "These customers are keeping me from getting my work done." In retrospect, I obviously missed the bigger picture.

Although it sounds cliché because we have read and heard it millions of times, development really is about relationships. As I addressed in the previous chapter, it is about serving the passions and interests of our customer—in this case the donor.

The quality and integrity of a donor relationship must always be allowed to trump the short-term needs of a nonprofit mission. For example, if it is June 22 and the nonprofit fiscal year ends June 30, is it appropriate to risk ruffling the feathers of a donor by pushing his or her decision in order to meet the fiscal year goal? No! No! And never!

Some quick backtracking here before I get in too much trouble. I am not saying it is right to ignore your boss or your board or your budgetary needs. What I am saying is that we must remember what we are trying to establish in the long run: long-term relationships that are fulfilling to both the donor and the nonprofit. Don't get too inwardly focused and miss this important point.

Challenge #4: Too Little Board Engagement

> *"It is no use walking anywhere to preach unless our walking is our preaching."*
>
> —St. Francis of Assisi

All too often, the extent of the board's involvement in a nonprofit organization is attending board meetings, and some don't even do that very well. To varying degrees, board members give in support of the mission. But few boards are challenged to understand or grasp the potential impact they could truly have on the mission.

Nearly all nonprofit-boards have some version of a job description that is shared with incoming members. On the board job descriptions, you will find very generic statements that could apply to almost any organization. And that is because it was probably copied from another organization, which was copied from another, and so on.

If there was only one generic statement on a board job description, it should be: **Leadership by example!**

This statement sums it up. Board members need to lead the way in every aspect of the organization that they want and expect others to follow. If they expect others to give, they should give; if they expect others to volunteer, they should volunteer; if they expect others to invite friends to give, they must be willing to invite friends to give.

Challenge #5: Too Little Prospect Prioritization

Are some donors more important than others? This is not a trick question! Most of us have two quick reactions: (1) Yes, of course, if someone has a jillion dollars (followed by a snicker) and (2) No, because the amount of money someone has shouldn't determine their value to a nonprofit.

At the risk of being controversial, the first answer is correct.

How can this be? Well, we first need to remember what our job is. I am going to walk out on a limb and guess that since you are reading this book, you have something to do with raising funds, whether you are a development director, board member, or a staff member who occasionally wears the fundraising hat. If we build on some of the previous chapters by agreeing that donors are customers and our job is to help fund the mission, then we should be able to conclude that people with wealth must be a priority.

In your fundraising role, you have a limited amount of time to give. Question: If you can only work with 15 prospective donors, which 15 do you choose? The 15 who could fund the entire mission if they were so inclined, or the 15 who could give you a collective $250? (FYI: If you answered the latter, then you are in the wrong role.)

Every mature and growing nonprofit organization learns this lesson—to segment donors into groups and assign resources to each group based on potential. The point is, if your job is to pan for gold, pan where the gold is.

I realize that most of the challenges defined in this chapter are inherent to the nonprofit and not the ideas of current development staff. Problems such as these are the result of compounded decisions made by many different boards and staff members over many years. And all of these leaders had the best intentions for the nonprofit.

It is, however, important to recognize these challenges as potential problems and impediments to long-term success. The goal of all development leaders must be to grow funding for the mission and leave the development operation better than you found it (because you won't be there forever). The first step in getting the development house in order is to throw out some of the old to make room for the new—assuming the new represents strategic, relationship-based activities.

Addressing these five common challenges will help you achieve your development goals as well as add to your wisdom about potential pitfalls in the future. Work them through and watch your efforts gain the success you've been looking for.

Chapter 16

The Bottom Line: A Thriving Mission

"The greatest danger for most of us is not that our aim is too high and we miss it, but that it is too low and we reach it."
—Michelangelo

We have covered much ground through the first fifteen chapters. I'm guessing the reason you made time to read this book is that you hoped to have a few takeaways to apply to your role as a staff member or volunteer for a nonprofit organization.

Although I do hope that you've found your reading worthwhile, from my perspective, success in fundraising doesn't come from a few new tasks and new ideas. Rather, it comes from adopting a philosophy and vision that reframe the way you *think* about fundraising. I often begin board-training meetings and seminars with a vision exercise intended to illustrate this very point. If you embrace the broader vision of the relationship-based approach and are willing to rethink the way you plan and execute your activities, then the small decisions are much easier to make.

The secret to dramatically growing operational funding or realizing significant capital for any nonprofit mission is to approach these challenges with caution, care, and concern. Think of it as you would if you were considering risking your own personal resources in a new business venture. Think like a customer by looking at everything you say and do from that perspective.

Far too many people who are otherwise intelligent and wise take fundraising for granted, believing it is easy to do and not worthy of significant time or investment. Statements like the following are spoken every day from nonprofit leaders:

- If people want to give, they will. We should not put pressure on them.

- Don't waste your time and money educating or motivating me—I will give what I can and that is that.

- If it is God's will, it will be.

- We don't have donors who can give large gifts.

- Let's take the amount we need and divide it by the number of donors we have to determine how much we need from each one.

- The most important objective is to get participation from every family.

- How hard can fundraising really be? Do we really need to pay someone that much to help us?

I believe the people who make these statements have the best intentions of helping their nonprofits succeed. But they probably live and work in a different world from the nonprofit sector and believe that nonprofit missions are more like hobbies or pastimes.

The reality? Fundraising is as important to a nonprofit organization as sales and revenue are to any for-profit corporation. And consider the lengths to which the for-profit world will go to ensure that sales are strong and investors receive a healthy return.

Nonprofit organizations require the same degree of strategic thought and planning as any for-profit corporation. And the consequences of not being savvy are just as significant. Annually, there are tens of thousands of nonprofits that fail having nothing to do with the relevance of their missions. It is due to the lack of funding.

If you are willing to invest some time into the financial well being of your nonprofit mission, then adopt the philosophy of *quality decisions* into your fundraising strategy and think like a donor. Apply the same care and concern to the business side of the organization as you would any other aspect of your life.

The secret to a thriving nonprofit mission is to ensure there is a growing source of funding. So, as Gandhi challenged us, "be the change you want to see in the world." Until we all start doing things differently, things will not change. Each of us are capable of transforming a mission that is important to us by focusing on a few quality donor decisions and serving their passions and interests. It is this engagement of a few donors that will redefine the way your entire team approaches development.

ACKNOWLEDGMENTS

Writing a book is much harder than I imagined and to say that I did it single handedly would be tossing those who are closest to me down the stairs. I have read countless industry books in my lifetime and always wondered how the authors found the time to produce such works. After working through this process over the past three years, I still wonder the same, but I am certain they did not do it alone.

Without question, there are two human driving forces in my life that disciplined me to complete this book. The first is my good friend and colleague, Sarah Landman. Sarah is one of my closest confidants and trusted advisors in my life. She is one of only two people in the world (the other being my wife) who is allowed to push me out of my comfort zone. It is Sarah's tenacity that is responsible for my part of the book actually getting finished.

The other driving force in my life is my wife Jennifer. I will save the reader from all the mushy stuff, and simply say that she is by far my greatest source of inspiration, helping me believe I can do anything, as well as the giver of a persistent dose of reality, reminding me that success should never go to my head.

Finally, to God be the glory for all good things that have come my way. It is to Him that I am the most appreciative for my life, family, friends, and salvation.

Made in the USA
San Bernardino, CA
02 March 2014